Penguin Books
Good Healthy Food

Gail Duff was born in Buckinghamshire and now lives in Kent with her photographer husband and small daughter, Lucy. Throughout her career as a broadcaster and cookery writer she has specialized in devising recipes which contain only natural foods. She has written many books on the subject including *Fresh All the Year*, *Gail Duff's Vegetarian Cookbook*, *The Good Housekeeping Wholefood Cookbook* and *Real Fast Food*. Her other interests are herbs, folklore and social history and on these subjects she has written *The Countryside Cookbook*, *Pot Pourri* and *Country Wisdom*. She has written for many publications including *Good Housekeeping*, *The Food Magazine*, *Parents* and the *Daily Telegraph* and in 1977 won the Glenfiddich Award for the best cookery writer of the year. Gail Duff is a frequent broadcaster on such programmes as 'Woman's Hour' and 'Tuesday Call', and she has appeared on 'Pebble Mill at One' and 'Look East' and various other regional television programmes.

Gail Duff

Good Healthy Food

Penguin Books

Penguin Books Ltd, Harmondsworth, Middlesex, England
Viking Penguin Inc., 40 West 23rd Street, New York, New York 10010, U.S.A.
Penguin Books Australia Ltd, Ringwood, Victoria, Australia
Penguin Books Canada Ltd, 2801 John Street, Markham, Ontario, Canada L3R 1B4
Penguin Books (N.Z.) Ltd, 182–190 Wairau Road, Auckland 10, New Zealand

First published 1985

Typeset in Linotron Trump Mediaeval by
Rowland Phototypesetting Ltd,
Bury St Edmunds, Suffolk
Printed and bound in Great Britain by
Cox & Wyman Ltd, Reading

For Valerie
with thanks for hard work and enthusiasm

Contents

Introduction

My main reason for writing about food is that I enjoy it. I get great pleasure from dreaming up recipes, testing them and finally eating the results. Another aspect that continues to fascinate me is the link between food and our general well-being. I am convinced that the better the quality of the food we eat, the healthier we are. By good quality, I don't mean expensive dishes from the best restaurants, but food prepared from fresh, natural ingredients. That, I suppose, is the definition of wholefood, and that, for me, is the ideal diet.

Various reports have recently been published about food and health and the information that has filtered down to most people is that we should eat more healthily. That is all very well, but what does 'more healthily' mean? Judging from the correspondence I receive, more than a few people are confused, and I am sure that because of the confusion some have given up on improving their diet before they have really begun.

The main conclusions of these reports are that we should take care over how much fat we consume and that in general we should be eating more vegetable fats, such as oils, and less animal fats, such as butter and the fat contained in meat. We should all be eating more fibre by way of wholewheat bread and pasta, brown rice and other grains, by using wholewheat flour in baking and, if possible, giving up white flour products altogether. Sugar should be an occasional treat rather than an everyday necessity and we should all cut down on salt, not only in cooking and on the table but also by eating fewer of the many processed foods that contain it.

A variety of fresh fruits and vegetables, both raw and cooked, should be eaten every day and we should experiment more with pulses and nuts and fish.

It is not my intention in this book to include further nutritional information. What I have tried to do in the following pages is to provide recipes for all occasions, using a wide range of ingredients in the best way possible. The recipes contain little or no fat, plenty of fibre, offer suggestions on how to cut down on sugar and the only salt used is when crushing garlic and cooking rice and pastas (although even this can be omitted if wished). All the recipes should be within the price range and experience of those people who enjoy the time that they spend in the kitchen and who wish to feed themselves and their family and friends well and healthily.

Because I want to encourage people to try healthier recipes, I have considered those who might just be starting to change their diet and have not included any unusual ingredients such as miso or tofu, good though they are. A few recipes call for tahini or for tamari sauce, both of which are available from large supermarkets, wholefood or health food shops, but I have worked mostly with familiar foods to show how they can be cooked and presented in healthier ways.

Another factor which may surprise some people is that the book is not vegetarian. It is quite possible to include meat in your diet provided that you do not eat it every day and that you are also eating a wide range of other foods which provide fibre and other vitamins and minerals. This will ensure that, even with meat, you can still regard your diet as a wholefood one.

I am not an extremist. If I fancy the odd blob of cream on my fruit or butter on my bread, then I have it, as I know that for most of the time my diet is as healthy as I can sensibly make it. Absolute rigidity when applied to diet or to any other aspect of daily life, can make us tense, anxious and miserable and these factors in themselves can cause illness.

If you are just thinking of changing over to healthier eating patterns, do so gradually. Sudden changes can upset both your digestive system and domestic harmony. First buy wholewheat bread instead of white and then gradually start baking with wholewheat flour. Introduce one salad meal in the week and replace one meat meal with one of fish or vegetarian ingredients. Take the salt off the table and then gradually cut down on its use in cooking. Serve a first course before the meal instead of a sugary sweet after, or make desserts with fresh and dried fruits. Later, experiment with sugar-free baking. One day you will look round and find that your store-cupboard contains only healthy ingredients, your cooking will have changed character and you and your family will be healthier. It could take a year or more but it will come in the end.

One thing I do hope is that you will still be enjoying your food. This book, written both for beginners and for seasoned healthy eaters who are searching for new recipes, is intended to help you to achieve all your aims.

Ingredients

Where necessary, I have described particular ingredients in their relevant chapters. Here is a short explanation of basic ingredients which are used throughout.

FATS AND OILS

In many of the recipes in this book, I have used only a small amount of fat or oils. You might be surprised to see that in some cases I have specified butter. I use it only in small amounts and maintain that if the only other added fat I eat in a day is oil in my salad dressing, and if I eat meat only four times a week, then I am allowed a thin scraping of butter on my home-made wholemeal bread or a tiny amount to soften the vegetables for soup. It is high in saturated fats, but a small amount mixed with plenty of other high fibre, low fat ingredients will do a healthy person no harm. If you wish, you can replace it in any recipe with a vegetable margarine.

When buying margarines, choose the soft types made only from vegetable fats. You can spread them and cook with them and they make cake and pastry making superbly easy.

I cook a great deal with oils and also use them in salad dressings. Buy specifically named oils such as olive, sunflower, safflower, soya, corn and groundnut. Where I have not specified a type of oil in a recipe, use any of these. Oils labelled simply 'vegetable oil' contain a mixture of cheap oils including rape and linseed and have poor flavour and nutritional quality. For special salads, buy what are called 'cold pressed oils' from wholefood shops. These have been obtained from the vegetables or nuts purely by pressing and not by chemical extraction. They are a deep amber colour and each has a distinct, nutty flavour. Keep them for salads as they are too expensive to use indiscriminately for cooking and besides may spit when heated.

FLOUR

Wherever flour is used in the book, it is always 100 per cent wholewheat, sometimes called wholemeal flour. This is produced from the whole of the wheat grain and contains fibre, vitamins and minerals. All supermarkets now stock it, as do small shops and wholefood shops.

SALT

I add salt to the water when boiling rice or pasta, use it for crushing garlic and put it into yeast recipes. I never add it to cooked dishes and never put it on the table. For cooking I use a sea salt, such as Maldon salt, or a natural rock salt. For crushing garlic, I very often substitute sesame salt. This consists of five parts sesame seeds to one of salt, which have been roasted and ground together. Use just a pinch and you can see how much it helps you to cut down on your salt intake without cutting down on the flavour. I have not mentioned it in the salad recipes, but if you can find it, use it.

Incidentally, if you think I have still included too much salt you can cut down even more or omit it altogether.

SWEETENERS

There is no fibre in any kind of sugar and all are very high in calories and little else although brown sugars contain very small amounts of vitamins and minerals. Sugar is not necessary in a healthy and well-balanced diet. It is far better to obtain calories from foods that also provide fibre and other nutrients. However, I have no wish to be a complete killjoy and in order to provide a happy balance of recipes I have included a little sugar in the desserts and baking sections, believing that although we should drastically cut down on our intake we cannot ban it altogether. The sugar that I use is Barbados. Nutritionists say that it is just as bad as white sugar but it does contain the B vitamins which we need in order to digest it properly. White sugar will simply deplete the body's supplies; brown sugar contains just enough to enable it to be digested without having to use up any more. Do not rely on it to provide you with vitamins, it won't, but at least it won't take any away. That is why I believe it is the lesser of two evils.

Molasses is a by-product of the sugar industry, containing all the goodness that is thrown away in the production of white sugar. It contains ten different minerals, significant amounts of some B vitamins and about two-thirds the calories of white sugar. Its only drawback is its strong flavour which you either love or hate. It is delicious in breads and cakes and can be added to fruit salads and cooked fruits.

Honey consists of seventy-five per cent sugars, mainly in the form of fructose or fruit sugar. Twenty per cent of it is water and the rest is made up from small amounts of vitamins A and C and some of those of the B group. It also contains small amounts of the mineral chromium, which aids the digestion of carbohydrates, and a substance called acetylcholine which helps to maintain a healthy blood pressure. Although some nutritionists would dismiss it along with white sugar as an unnecessary constituent of our diet, I would say that small amounts will do no harm in a healthy diet.

YOGHURT

There are many different varieties of natural yoghurt, each with its own particular flavour. Try them all and choose which you like best.

To make your own yoghurt, either use a yoghurt-maker with instructions provided or a wide-necked vacuum flask. Skimmed milk and ordinary pasteurized can successfully be made into yoghurt; long life and sterilized milks give a very firm set. I prefer to use goat's milk as I like the nutty flavour. Put the milk into a saucepan and bring it gently to the boil. Let it boil until it rises up the sides of the pan. Cool it to 115°F (46°C). Put 1 tbsp natural yoghurt per pint (575 ml) milk into a large bowl. Gradually stir in the milk to make a smooth mixture. Pour the mixture into a wide-necked vacuum flask and leave it undisturbed for 8 hours. Transfer the yoghurt to pots, cover and refrigerate immediately. If you find yoghurt made from skimmed or pasteurized milk rather liquid, add 1 tbsp skimmed milk powder to the yoghurt in the bowl before stirring in the milk.

If yoghurt is added to a boiling liquid it will curdle. Therefore, if you are going to add it to dishes while they are still cooking it is best to stabilize it. To do this, put half an uncooked egg white or ½ tbsp cornflour into a small saucepan. Stir in ½ pint (275 ml) natural yoghurt and stir until the mixture boils. Simmer gently for 10 minutes, stirring frequently. Cool and put into a covered container. Stabilized yoghurt will keep in the refrigerator for up to a week.

A Typical Day's Healthy Eating

BREAKFAST

Choose any one or more of the following:
Natural fruit juice
Fresh fruit or soaked dried fruits with natural yoghurt
Meusli or another whole grain cereal, preferably sugar-free
Wholewheat toast or crispbreads with very little butter or vegetable margarine
Grilled tomatoes or mushrooms on wholewheat toast
On one or two days in the week, a boiled egg with wholewheat toast.

Wholewheat pancakes are a good substitute for bread or toast on some days.

LIGHT MEAL

Make this a salad meal. Make a large salad including a wide variety of raw vegetables, add a few nuts or cooked beans if required or serve with a low fat cheese. Accompany with wholewheat bread or crispbreads or a jacket baked potato.

Follow with fresh fruit or dried fruits if required.

LARGE MEAL

Serve a hot, high protein dish consisting of fish, meat or a vegetarian savoury. Include a selection of fresh vegetables plus potatoes, pasta or grains.

Either begin with a soup or light starter or follow with a wholefood sweet.

BETWEEN MEALS

You may well find that once you are used to a wholefood diet, you will not get hunger pangs between meals. If you do, nibble fresh fruit or vegetables such as carrots and celery cut into small sticks. Or eat wholewheat biscuits (plain or semi-sweet); meusli bars; nuts; dried fruits; fruit bars.

If your between meals snacks start to spoil your appetite, then try to cut down on them.

NOTES

All recipes serve four people unless otherwise stated.
1 tsp = 5 ml; 1 tbsp = 15 ml.

Planning Wholefood Meals

We all know that meals should be balanced and most of us do it by instinct. The aim is not to have too much of one particular ingredient and to vary your cooking methods and presentation. Choose a wide variety of ingredients and cooking methods and you will add both to enjoyment and to nutritional value. For example, if the main dish is going to be rich and heavy it is not a good idea to serve a thick, rich soup to begin with. A fruit-based or salad starter would be much more appropriate. Then, if you begin with fresh fruit, something like a fruit salad as a sweet would probably be too much of a good thing. If the main dish is a casserole containing vegetables, then a salad would be a better accompaniment than a selection of cooked vegetables.

If possible, vary colours and textures as well. Make one part of the meal crunchy, another smooth and another grainy. Serve different coloured vegetables together such as carrots, spinach and celery, rather than several different green ones.

Besides providing variety in one meal, try to remember what was served at other mealtimes during the day and make them all slightly different. Then go on to change things from day to day. Serve meat or fish one day, a hot vegetarian dish on another and perhaps a main course salad dish on the next. This way, you will be serving the widest variety of nutrients possible.

Soups

Soup makes a warming start to any meal and can be served all the year round. Make it thick and warming in winter, and in summer make it with light summer vegetables such as cucumber or marrow.

At lunch or supper time, or at any time when you want only a light meal, a bowl of soup can be scattered with grated cheese or chopped nuts and served with wholewheat bread and perhaps a side salad.

The essential ingredient in any soup, be it hot or cold, thick or clear, is well-made stock. It takes very little trouble to make your own and it will be so much better in flavour than the best of bought cubes, all of which tend to be over-salted.

You can make stock using meat as a base or purely with vegetable ingredients. My basic stock that is always in the refrigerator is based on chicken giblets or a chicken quarter. It is light brown in colour and I find I can use it with all ingredients from beef to beans. If you prefer to keep your bean and lentil dishes and vegetable soups purely vegetarian, then make the vegetable stock.

When making thick soups I usually rely solely on the vegetables for thickening, rarely using milk and never cream. Natural yoghurt will give a creamy texture and a light, slightly sharp flavour; and curd cheese thickens and flavours without making the soup over-rich. Soured cream can be used as a garnish or added to light soups such as cucumber. I add wholewheat flour to some clear soups to give a little more body.

You will probably notice that most of the recipes begin by softening the vegetables in a little butter. This method gives a richer texture and flavour and ½ oz (15 g) between four people is not a lot. You can use a soft, vegetable margarine instead if you wish. An alternative method would be to simmer the vegetables in a very little stock until all the stock has been absorbed and then carry on as given with the recipe after softening.

CHICKEN STOCK

> 1 set chicken giblets (liver removed),
>   or 1 chicken portion, or 4 chicken wing tips
> 1 onion, halved not peeled
> 1 large carrot, halved lengthways
> 1 celery stick, broken into three
> few celery leaves
> 2 tsp black peppercorns
> 2 bayleaves
> bouquet garni

This is the basic formula. To this you can add any other vegetable trimmings such as potato peelings, root vegetable trimmings, the stalks of spring greens.

Into the largest saucepan you have (12 pints/7 l is about right) put the chicken pieces, plus all the other basic ingredients. Set them on a very low heat and stir occasionally until the chicken pieces and the vegetables brown. Pour in cold water to come about 1½ inches (4 cm) from the top of the pan. Bring to the boil. Add any other vegetables that you may be using. Simmer very gently, uncovered, for 1½ hours, skimming as and when necessary.

Cool the stock slightly. Strain it into a plastic container and leave it until it is completely cold. Cover tightly and store near the top of the refrigerator. It should keep for up to a week.

Once you have made your stock you will come to rely on it and want to keep a constant supply in the refrigerator. Your weekly boil-up should become part of your kitchen routine.

VEGETABLE STOCK

This has a similar colour to the chicken stock and is very well flavoured provided that you use a good mixture of fresh vegetables.

> *Essential ingredients:*
> 2 medium onions, halved not peeled
> 2 medium carrots, halved lengthways
> 2 celery sticks, broken
> few celery leaves
> trimmings from dark green cabbage, spring greens,
>   kale or brussels sprouts

2 bayleaves
bouquet garni
2 tsp black peppercorns
2 tbsp tamari or soy sauce

Extra ingredients (if possible half-fill the saucepan with
these):
root vegetable trimmings, e.g. potato, celeriac,
    swede, turnip, parsnip
trimmed ends of leeks
cauliflower stalks
brussels sprouts trimmings
outer pieces of runner beans
pea and bean pods

Put all the ingredients into a 12 pint (7 l) saucepan. Add any
liquid left over from cooking white beans (brown bean stock is
too bitter). Pour in water to about 1½ inches (4 cm) from the top
of the pan. Bring to the boil and simmer, uncovered, for 2 hours.

Cool. Strain into a plastic container and cover tightly when
cold. Keep the stock near the top of the refrigerator and it will
stay fresh for up to a week.

Artichoke and Apple Soup

The apple used here does not have a strong taste, but it just
lightens the smoky-flavoured artichokes.

1 lb (450 g) Jerusalem artichokes
1 really large Bramley apple
½ oz (15 g) butter
1 large onion, quartered and thinly sliced
1½ pints (850 ml) stock
bouquet garni including a sprig of sage
sea salt and freshly ground black pepper
4 tbsp soured cream

Peel the artichokes, keeping them in a bowl of cold water to
which you have added a dash of white wine vinegar or lemon
juice. Slice them thinly. Peel, core and thinly slice the apple.

Melt the butter in a saucepan over a low heat. Mix in the

artichokes, apple and onion. Cover and cook them gently for 10 minutes. Pour in the stock and bring to the boil. Add the bouquet garni and season. Cover and simmer for 30 minutes.

Remove the bouquet garni and either work the soup in a blender or food processor until it is smooth or rub it through the fine blade of a vegetable mill. Reheat if necessary and serve in individual bowls with 1 tsp of soured cream blobbed on top of each.

Avocado and Tomato Soup

Avocado soup is always smooth and creamy and very simple to make.

> 2 avocados, ripe but firm
> 8 oz (225 g) tomatoes
> 4 tbsp oil
> 1 large onion, finely chopped
> 1 pint (575 ml) stock
> bouquet garni
> 1 clove garlic, crushed with a pinch sea salt

Peel and stone the avocados. Mash one to a purée and finely chop the other. Scald, skin and chop the tomatoes. Heat the oil in a saucepan over a low heat. Add the onion and cook until it is soft. Add the tomatoes, cover and cook for 5 minutes. Pour in the stock and bring to the boil. Add the bouquet garni, cover and simmer for 10 minutes.

Remove the bouquet garni. Put the contents of the pan into a blender or food processor with the avocado purée and crushed garlic and work until you have a smooth soup. Reheat gently without boiling. Pour into individual bowls and float the chopped avocado on top.

Alternative: chill the soup after blending and float chopped basil on the top with the avocado pieces.

Broad Bean and Onion Soup

This is a really simple summer soup, full of flavour and with a slight lemony tang to lighten it.

    1 large onion
    2 lb (900 g) broad beans (weighed before shelling)
    ½ oz (15 g) butter
    1 tbsp flour
    1½ pints (850 ml) stock
    1 tbsp chopped savory
    1 tbsp chopped thyme
    juice 1 lemon

Finely chop the onion. Shell and finely chop the beans. Melt the butter in a saucepan over a low heat, stir in the onion and soften it. Stir in the beans, cover the pan and cook gently for 5 minutes.

Stir in the flour and then the stock. Bring gently to the boil, stirring. Add the herbs and lemon juice and simmer gently, uncovered, for 20 minutes.

Carrot, Cauliflower and Cheese Soup

This is a pretty, soft coloured soup, creamy in texture but low in calories.

    1 small cauliflower
    6 oz (175 g) carrots
    1 medium onion, thinly sliced
    1½ pints (850 ml) stock
    freshly ground black pepper
    1 bayleaf
    2 oz (50 g) curd cheese
    1 small clove garlic, crushed with a pinch sea salt
    2 tbsp chopped parsley

Chop the cauliflower into small pieces and slice the carrots thinly. Put them into a saucepan with the onion and stock.

Season with the pepper and add the bayleaf. Cover, bring to the boil and simmer for 30 minutes.

Remove the bayleaf and put the rest into a blender with the cheese and garlic. Work them until you have a smooth, pale salmon pink soup.

Return it to the saucepan, stir in the parsley and reheat.

Creamy Carrot and Swede Soup

Leaving a portion of a thick soup unblended gives it an interesting, chunky texture.

> 1 lb (450 g) swede
> 6 oz (175 g) carrots
> 1 large onion
> ½ oz (15 g) butter
> 1½ pints (850 ml) stock
> bouquet garni
> sea salt and freshly ground black pepper
> 3 tbsp soured cream

Dice the vegetables into very small, even sized pieces. Melt the butter in a saucepan over a low heat. Stir in the vegetables, cover and let them sweat for 10 minutes. Pour in the stock and bring to the boil. Put in the bouquet garni and season. Cover and simmer for 20 minutes.

Remove the bouquet garni. Put two-thirds of the soup into a blender and work it until it is smooth. Stir it into the rest and add the soured cream.

Reheat the soup gently before serving.

Celeriac and Bacon Soup

Celeriac is a much neglected vegetable that has a creamy texture when cooked and the flavour of celery. Bacon and sage are perfect accompaniments.

> 1 lb (450 g) celeriac
> ½ oz (15 g) butter

1 large onion, finely chopped
4 oz (125 g) lean bacon, diced
1½ pints (850 ml) stock
bouquet of sage leaves
2 tbsp chopped celery leaves (if available),
    or chopped parsley

Peel and finely chop the celeriac. Melt the butter in a heavy saucepan over a low heat. Stir in the celeriac, onion and bacon. Cover and cook gently for 10 minutes. Pour in the stock and bring it to the boil. Add the sage. Cover and simmer for 20 minutes.

Remove the sage. Cool the mixture slightly and work it in a blender or food processor until it is smooth; or put it through a vegetable mill.

Reheat the soup. Pour into individual bowls and scatter the celery leaves or parsley over the top.

Celery and Mustard Soup

This is a light, spicy soup. The wine can be omitted if preferred:

12 oz (350 g) celery
1 large onion
½ oz (15 g) butter
1 tbsp wholewheat flour
1½ pints (850 ml) stock
bouquet garni
1 tbsp spiced granular mustard (preferably one
    containing white wine)
4 tbsp dry white wine (optional)
4 tbsp chopped parsley

Finely chop the celery and onion. Melt the butter in a saucepan over a low heat and stir in the celery and onion. Cover and cook gently for 5 minutes. Stir in the flour and then the stock. Bring the soup to the boil, stirring. Add the bouquet garni and simmer, uncovered, for 20 minutes.

Remove the bouquet garni. Stir in the mustard, wine and parsley and simmer for a further 2 minutes.

Cucumber and Mint Soup

This is a light summer soup that is equally good served either hot or chilled.

>   1 large cucumber
>   ½ oz (15 g) butter
>   1 large onion, finely chopped
>   1 clove garlic, finely chopped
>   1½ pints (850 ml) stock
>   2 sprigs mint
>   ¼ pint (150 ml) soured cream
>   2 tbsp chopped mint

Wipe the cucumber but do not peel it. Cut it into quarters lengthways and remove the seeds. Finely chop it. Melt the butter in a saucepan over a low heat. Stir in the cucumber (reserving 2 tbsp for garnish), onion and garlic. Cover the pan and cook gently for 10 minutes. Pour in the stock and add the sprigs of mint. Simmer for 10 minutes, covered.

   Remove the mint. Work the soup in a blender or food processor until it is smooth. Return the soup to the pan and stir in the soured cream and the chopped mint. Reheat gently without boiling, or chill completely. When chilled, pour into soup bowls (it looks perfect in glass ones) and float the reserved cucumber on the top.

Cucumber, Tomato and Spring Onion Soup

In complete contrast to the previous recipe, this cucumber soup is deep red and richly flavoured.

>   1 small cucumber
>   1 lb (450 g) ripe tomatoes
>   10 medium spring onions
>   ½ oz (15 g) butter

1 clove garlic, finely chopped
¾ pint (425 ml) stock
¼ pint (150 ml) sherry
1 tbsp tomato purée
2 tbsp chopped parsley

Wipe and finely chop the cucumber. Scald, skin and chop the tomatoes. Chop the spring onions. Melt the butter in a saucepan over a low heat. Stir in the cucumber, tomatoes, spring onions and garlic. Cover and leave them for 10 minutes.

Pour in the stock and sherry and stir in the tomato purée. Cover again and simmer for 20 minutes. Stir in the parsley just before serving.

Green Grape Soup

This is an unusual, delicately flavoured soup for a special occasion.

2 medium onions
½ oz (15 g) butter
1 tbsp wholewheat flour
1¼ pints (725 ml) stock
4 oz (125 g) curd cheese
1 glass (5 fl oz) dry white wine
6 oz (175 g) green grapes, halved and seeded

Finely chop the onions. Melt the butter in a saucepan over a low heat. Stir in the onions and soften them. Stir in the flour and then the stock. Bring to the boil, stirring, and simmer uncovered for 10 minutes.

Cream the cheese in a bowl with a wooden spoon and gradually work in about ½ pint (275 ml) of the soup. Stir the resulting mixture back into the saucepan. Add the wine and prepared grapes and reheat gently without boiling.

Very unusual but very effective.

Leek and Green Pepper Soup

This is a thick, chunky and very savoury soup.

> 12 oz (350 g) leeks
> 2 oz (50 g) lean bacon
> ½ oz (15 g) butter
> 1 large green pepper
> 1 tbsp wholewheat flour
> 1½ pints (850 ml) stock
> 1 bayleaf
> 1 tbsp chopped parsley
> 1 tbsp chopped marjoram

Thinly slice the leeks and dice the bacon. Melt the butter in a large heavy saucepan over a low heat and stir in the leeks and bacon. Cook gently, stirring occasionally, until the leeks are soft.

Meanwhile, finely chop the green pepper. Stir the flour and then the stock into the leeks. Bring the soup gently to the boil, stirring. Add the bayleaf, pepper and herbs. Simmer very gently, uncovered, for 15 minutes.

Marrow and Tomato Soup

Yoghurt is a perfect ingredient in marrow soups as it adds extra creaminess.

> 1 small marrow weighing about 1½ lbs (675 g)
> ½ oz (15 g) butter
> 1 large onion, thinly sliced
> 1 lb (450 g) ripe tomatoes
> 1 pint (575 ml) stock
> bouquet garni
> ¼ pint (150 ml) natural yoghurt
> 2 tbsp chopped basil or parsley

Peel, seed and thinly slice the marrow. Melt the butter in a saucepan over a low heat. Stir in the marrow and onion, cover and cook gently for 5 minutes. Scald, skin and chop the tomatoes and stir them into the pan. Cover again and cook for a further 5 minutes. Pour in the stock and bring to the boil. Add the bouquet garni, cover and simmer for 15 minutes.

Remove the bouquet garni. Work in a blender or food processor until you have a smooth, pale orange soup. Add the yoghurt and blend for a few seconds more. Return the soup to a clean saucepan. Stir in the basil or parsley and reheat without boiling.

Mushroom and Chervil Soup

If you can use field mushrooms for this, do so. They come into season just as the second crop of chervil shoots up in the herb garden. Together, they make a superb soup which is creamy and warming for chilly autumn evenings. Parsley can be used if chervil is not available.

> 8 oz (225 g) open mushrooms
> 1 oz (25 g) butter
> 2 medium onions, finely chopped
> 1 tbsp wholewheat flour
> 1½ pints (850 ml) stock
> 3 tbsp chopped chervil, or parsley
> juice ½ lemon

Finely chop the mushrooms. Melt the butter in a saucepan over a low heat. Mix in the mushrooms and onions. Cover and cook gently for 10 minutes. Stir in the flour and cook for ½ minute. Stir in the stock and bring to the boil. Add 2 tbsp of the chervil and simmer gently, uncovered, for 15 minutes.

Work the soup in a blender or food processor or put it through a vegetable mill. Return it to the saucepan and stir in the lemon juice and remaining chervil. Reheat to serve.

Green Pea, Carrot and Lettuce Soup

You don't need any other herbs for this soup provided you have the sorrel. If you haven't any, add a sprig of mint when you simmer the vegetables, but remove it before sieving or blending. Then garnish the soup when you serve it with chopped parsley.

>   8 oz (225 g) green peas (weighed before shelling)
>   8 oz (225 g) new carrots
>   1 small round lettuce
>   8 sorrel leaves (see above)
>   ½ oz (15 g) butter
>   1½ pints (850 ml) stock

Shell the peas, thinly slice the carrots and chop the lettuce and sorrel. Melt the butter in a saucepan over a low heat, stir in the peas and carrots, cover them and cook gently for 5 minutes.

Stir in the stock and bring to the boil. Add the lettuce and sorrel. Cover the pan and let everything simmer for 20 minutes. Cool the soup slightly and work it in a blender or food processor or put it through the medium blade of a vegetable mill. Return the soup to the pan and reheat gently before serving.

Creamed Pumpkin and Carrot Soup

Pumpkin always makes creamy golden soups.

>   1½ lbs (675 g) chopped pumpkin, weighed after
>   peeling and seeding
>   8 oz (225 g) carrots
>   ½ oz (15 g) butter
>   1 large onion
>   ½ pint (275 ml) stock
>   1 pint (575 ml) milk
>   2 tbsp tomato purée
>   bouquet garni
>   freshly ground black pepper
>   2 tbsp chopped parsley

Finely chop the pumpkin, carrots and onion. Melt the butter in a saucepan over a low heat. Add the pumpkin, carrots and onion. Cover and cook them gently for 10 minutes. Pour in the stock and milk and bring to the boil. Stir in the tomato purée, add the bouquet garni and season with the pepper. Cover and simmer for 20 minutes.

Remove the bouquet garni and either work the soup in a blender or food processor until it is smooth or put it through a vegetable mill. Return the soup to the saucepan, stir in the parsley and reheat.

Spinach and Spring Onion Soup

This unthickened soup is light but packed full of spinach and onions.

> 1 lb (450 g) spinach
> 12 large spring onions
> ½ oz (15 g) butter
> 1½ pints (850 ml) stock
> 4 oz (125 g) curd cheese
> 4 tbsp chopped parsley

Wash and finely chop the spinach. Chop the spring onions. Melt the butter in a saucepan over a low heat. Stir in the spinach and onions, cover and cook them gently for 10 minutes. Stir in the stock, bring to the boil, cover and simmer for 10 minutes. Take the pan from the heat.

Cream the cheese in a bowl and gradually work in ¼ pint (150 ml) of the hot soup. Stir the cheese mixture back into the saucepan, add the parsley and reheat the soup without boiling.

Tomato Soup with Smoked Mackerel

This is a bit like a fish gazpacho with a rich tomato flavour.

> 1 lb (450 g) ripe tomatoes
> 3 oz (75 g) smoked mackerel fillet
> 1 large green pepper

    4 tbsp oil
    1 large onion, finely chopped
    1 clove garlic, finely chopped
    1 tsp paprika
    ¼ pint (150 ml) dry white wine
    2 tbsp chopped basil or parsley

Scald, skin and roughly chop the tomatoes. Skin and flake the mackerel. Core, seed and finely chop the pepper.

    Heat the oil in a saucepan over a low heat. Mix in the pepper, onion and garlic. Cover and cook them gently for 15 minutes. Add the paprika and tomatoes, cover again and cook for a further 10 minutes until the tomatoes are soft. Mix in the mackerel, wine, basil and ¼ pt (150 ml) water. Bring the soup to the boil and simmer gently for 15 minutes.

Turnip and Apple Salad Soup

If you fancy a sharp taste and almost raw vegetables on a cold night, try this instead of a salad.

    3 tbsp oil
    1 medium onion, finely chopped
    8 oz (225 g) turnips, grated
    1 large cooking apple, cored and very finely chopped
    1½ pints (850 ml) stock
    1 tbsp grated horseradish
    2 tbsp cider vinegar
    2 tbsp soured cream

Heat the oil in a saucepan over a low heat, add the onion and soften it. Stir in the turnip and apple and pour in the stock. Bring to the boil and simmer for 2 minutes.

    Stir in the horseradish, vinegar and cream. Reheat if necessary, without boiling, to serve.

Thick Vegetable Soup

This is a good thick soup for winter.

>   8 large celery sticks
>   8 oz (225 g) carrots
>   8 oz (225 g) tomatoes
>   8 oz (225 g) potatoes
>   1 large onion
>   1 pint (575 ml) stock
>   bouquet garni
>   sea salt and freshly ground black pepper
>   ¼ pint (150 ml) natural yoghurt
>   1 clove garlic, crushed with a pinch sea salt (optional)

Finely chop the celery and carrots. Scald, skin and chop the tomatoes. Peel and chop the potatoes. Finely chop the onion. Put the stock into a large saucepan and bring it to the boil. Add the vegetables and bouquet garni and season. Cover and simmer for 20 minutes.

Remove the bouquet garni. Work the soup in a blender or food processor until smooth. Add the yoghurt and garlic and blend again.

Reheat gently, if necessary, without boiling.

First Courses

I always enjoy a first course. I find that it wakes up the taste buds and tantalizes the appetite. That is, if it is made from fresh ingredients and is not too large and heavy. A meal made up of first course and main course can be healthier than one consisting of a main course and a sweet, so if you have always thought of a first course as being rather a luxury, why not give it a try?

Most of my first courses, whether hot or cold, are based on vegetables and fruits, and I like them to complement the dishes of the main meal. If, for example, I am serving cooked vegetables with the main dish, then I would choose a small, prettily arranged salad or perhaps some fresh fruits topped with a garlic-flavoured natural yogurt as a good first course. If I am serving a hot dish with a green salad, a suitable first course would be grilled vegetables, such as aubergine or courgette slices, or cooked sweetcorn with cheese.

For special occasions, I look for the more exotic. Globe artichokes look and taste superb and are well worth the slightly longer preparation time. Avocados can be served plain or made into dips and pâtés. Mangoes, pineapples and watermelons all make first courses that are fresh and simple.

Fish and shellfish also make attractive first courses. I tend to keep these for special occasions and serve them before lightly cooked meat dishes or vegetarian main courses.

Grilled Apples with Ham and Cheese

Melting apples with a scattering of ham and cheese give a taste of traditional country fare.

> 2 large cooking apples
> 2 tbsp oil
> 1 tsp dried sage, crumbled

2 oz (50 g) cooked lean ham, finely chopped
2 oz (50 g) farmhouse Cheddar cheese, grated

Peel, quarter and core the apples and cut them into thin length-ways slices. Arrange the slices on 4 small heatproof plates. Brush them with the oil and scatter a little sage over them. Heat the grill to high.

Put the apples under the heat until they begin to soften and sizzle (about 1½ minutes). Scatter the ham over the apples and cover with the cheese. Return the apples to the heat and serve just as the cheese is melting and before it starts to bubble or brown.

Globe Artichokes with Parsley Dressing

Globe artichokes are always impressive and fun to eat, but serve them only when you have time for a leisurely meal.

4 globe artichokes
juice 1 lemon
1 large bouquet parsley

Dressing
¼ pint (150 ml) natural yoghurt
2 tsp tahini (sesame paste)
2 tbsp olive oil
1 clove garlic, crushed with a pinch sea salt
freshly ground black pepper
6 tbsp chopped parsley

Trim the artichokes. Bring a large pan of water to the boil and add half the lemon juice and the bouquet of parsley. Add the artichokes and boil them for 45 minutes.

To make the dressing, beat the yoghurt with the remaining lemon juice, tahini, oil, garlic and pepper. Mix in the parsley.

Drain the artichokes and remove the chokes. Serve them on large plates, with the dressing in a separate dish.

Curried Lemon Aubergines

Aubergines always make very satisfying first courses, even when they are simply grilled and served alone.

> 4 small aubergines
> 1 tbsp sea salt
> 4 fl oz (125 ml) olive oil
> juice 1 lemon
> ½ tsp hot Madras curry powder
> 2 tsp cumin seeds
> ¼ pint (150 ml) natural yoghurt

Cut the aubergines into ⅜ inch (1 cm) thick slices. Put them into a colander, sprinkle with sea salt and leave to drain for 30 minutes. Rinse them under cold water and dry with kitchen paper.

Beat the rest of the ingredients (except the yoghurt) together. Brush the aubergine slices on both sides with the curry mixture. Heat the grill to high. Lay the aubergine slices on the hot rack and grill them for 2 minutes on each side.

Serve hot, with the yoghurt spooned over the top.

Aubergine and Courgette Kebabs

> 8 oz (225 g) aubergine
> 1 tbsp sea salt
> 8 oz (225 g) courgettes
> 4 tbsp oil
> 2 tbsp white wine vinegar
> 1 tbsp tomato purée
> 1 tsp ground paprika
> ½ tsp ground cinnamon
> pinch chilli powder
> 1 clove garlic, crushed with a pinch sea salt

Cut the aubergines into 1 inch (2.5 cm) dice. Put them into a colander, sprinkle with sea salt and leave to drain for 30 minutes. Rinse them under cold water and dry with kitchen paper.

Cut the courgettes into 1 inch (2.5 cm) dice. Beat the remaining ingredients together. Fold in the aubergines and courgettes and leave them to marinate for 2 hours at room temperature.

Thread the vegetables on to kebab skewers. Heat the grill to high. Grill the kebabs, turning once, until the vegetables soften and begin to brown – about 5 minutes.

Grilled Avocados with Olives

Serve avocados hot for a change, filled with sizzling black olives.

>   2 ripe avocados
>   16 black olives
>   4 tbsp olive oil
>   1 tbsp lemon juice, or white wine vinegar
>   1 clove garlic, crushed with a pinch sea salt
>   freshly ground black pepper

Halve and stone the avocados. Halve and stone the olives and put 4 into the hollow of each avocado. Beat the remaining ingredients together to make the dressing. Place the avocados in a shallow heatproof dish. Spoon the dressing over the top. Put the avocados under a preheated grill for 4 minutes or until the dressing begins to bubble.

Mushrooms in Sherry

Sherry makes a good rich sauce for mushrooms, but for a cheaper meal use the juice of ½ lemon made up to ¼ pint (150 ml) with stock.

>   8 oz (225 g) button mushrooms
>   2 green peppers
>   4 tbsp olive oil
>   1 medium onion, thinly sliced
>   1 clove garlic, finely chopped

¼ pint (150 ml) dry sherry (see above)
1 tbsp tomato purée
4 tbsp chopped parsley

Keep the mushrooms whole. Core and seed the peppers and cut them into pieces 1 × ¼ inch (2.5 cm × 6 mm). Heat the oil in a frying pan over a low heat. Add the onion, garlic and peppers. Cook until the onion is soft.

Raise the heat and add the mushrooms. Cook for 2 minutes, stirring. Pour in the sherry (or lemon juice and stock) and bring to the boil. Mix in the tomato purée and cook until the liquid in the pan has reduced by half.

Serve hot, scattered with parsley and accompanied by whole-wheat bread.

Pumpkin Slices with Tomato Sauce

Pumpkin is a delicious vegetable, but very seasonal. When it is not available, the same sauce can be used for steamed sliced courgettes or marrow rings.

four ¼ inch (6 mm) slices from a medium pumpkin
bouquet garni
12 oz (350 g) ripe tomatoes
2 tbsp oil
1 medium onion, finely chopped
1 large clove garlic, finely chopped
2 tsp molasses
4 tsp malt vinegar
1 tbsp chopped basil or thyme

Cut all the pith from the pumpkin slices but leave the rind so that they hold their shape during cooking. Put them into a vegetable steamer if you have one large enough, or a colander in a large saucepan covered with a lid or foil. Tuck in the bouquet garni and steam the slices for 15 minutes, turning them once.

Make the sauce while the pumpkin slices are cooking. Scald, skin and roughly chop the tomatoes. Put the oil into a saucepan and set it on a low heat. Stir in the onion and garlic, cover and cook them for 5 minutes. Stir in the tomatoes, cover again and cook for a further 5 minutes. Mash the mixture well to make a pulpy purée and stir in the molasses, vinegar and chopped herbs. Simmer uncovered for a further 2 minutes.

Put the slices of pumpkin on to 4 plates and spoon the sauce over the top. Serve as a warming first course with brown toast.

Sweetcorn, Spring Onions and Cheese

This is a very substantial first course. Serve it before a light meal.

> 2 corn cobs
> 12 spring onions
> 1 oz (25 g) butter
> 4 oz (125 g) grated farmhouse Cheddar cheese
> 2 tbsp chopped parsley

Cut the corn from the cobs and chop the spring onions. Melt the butter in a saucepan over a low heat. Stir in the corn and onions. Cover them and set them on a very low heat for 15 minutes, stirring once or twice. Fold in the cheese and parsley and put the mixture into 4 small, warm serving bowls.

Arrange fingers of wholewheat toast around the edges to serve.

Grilled Tomatoes with Peanut Butter

This dish is simple to make but delicious to eat. If white wine isn't available, use orange juice instead.

> 1 lb (450 g) firm sweet tomatoes
> 4 tbsp crunchy peanut butter
> 3 tbsp dry white wine (see above)
> watercress or mustard and cress to garnish

Cut the tomatoes in half crossways. Put the peanut butter into a bowl and gradually work in the wine. Spread the mixture on top of the tomatoes. Heat the grill to moderate and cook the tomatoes at a small distance from the heat until the tops are brown.

Serve the tomatoes on wholewheat or granary toast, or have a plate of toast to hand round separately. Garnish with the watercress or mustard and cress just before serving.

Prawns Baked with Tomatoes

Serve prawns for a special occasion. Cooked this way they are light and appetizing.

> 8 oz (225 g) shelled prawns
> 1 tsp paprika
> pinch cayenne pepper
> 4 medium tomatoes
> 4 tbsp natural yoghurt

Preheat the oven to 400°F (200°C/gas 6). Divide the prawns between 4 small soufflé dishes and sprinkle them with paprika and cayenne pepper. Scald, skin and chop the tomatoes and put them on top of the prawns.

Put the dishes into the oven for 10 minutes so the prawns and tomatoes heat through but don't overcook. Add 1 tbsp of natural yoghurt and a sprinkling of paprika to each dish. Place the hot dishes on small plates before serving. Eat the prawns with a teaspoon.

Mushroom and Watercress Dip

Mushrooms and a low fat cheese make a rich tasting but low caloried dip.

> 6 oz (175 g) flat mushrooms
> 1 large onion
> 3 oz (75 g) watercress
> 1 oz (25 g) butter
> juice ½ lemon

4 oz (125 g) fromage blanc
2 large carrots
½ cucumber
1 red pepper
4 celery sticks

Finely chop the mushrooms, onion and watercress. Melt the butter in a frying pan over a low heat. Stir in the mushrooms and onion. Cover and cook gently for 10 minutes. Add the watercress and lemon juice. Cover again and cook for a further 2 minutes.

Cool the mixture. Put it into a blender or food processor with the cheese and work it to a smooth purée. Chill the dip for 1 hour.

Divide the dip between 4 small dishes. Cut the vegetables into small sticks. Place each dish in the centre of a large plate and surround it with the vegetable sticks. Serve with wholewheat toast or biscuits.

Avocado, Tuna and Cheese Mould

This luxury first course will serve 8. You could also serve it as a light meal for 4.

2 ripe avocados
2 7 oz (200 g) tins tuna
8 oz (225 g) curd cheese
grated rind and juice ½ lemon
freshly ground black pepper
oil for greasing
6 tbsp chopped parsley
6 black olives

Peel, stone and mash the avocados. Drain and flake the tuna. Mix the tuna and cheese into the avocados and pound them well together – a potato masher is a good implement for this. Mix in the lemon rind and juice and pepper. Press the mixture into an oiled 2 lb (900 g) loaf tin. Place in the refrigerator for 1 hour to firm.

Turn the mould on to a plate and press the parsley over the top and sides. Halve and stone the olives and arrange the halves down the centre of the mould.

Grapefruit, Banana and Walnut Salad

Bananas mashed with vinegar make a creamy sweet-and-sour dressing.

> 2 medium grapefruit
> 2 oz (50 g) shelled walnuts, chopped
> 2 ripe bananas
> 2 tbsp cider vinegar
> 1 clove garlic, crushed with a pinch sea salt
> freshly ground black pepper
> 4 walnut halves to garnish

Halve the grapefruit. Cut the flesh from the shells, leaving the shells intact. Chop the flesh and mix it with the walnuts. Pile it back into the shells.

Mash the bananas with the vinegar, garlic and pepper and spoon them over the top. Garnish each salad with a walnut half.

Tropical Yoghurt Salad

This is a colourful and refreshing starter with sharp, sweet sherbety flavours blended together.

> 2 mangoes
> two ½ inch (1.5 cm) thick slices pineapple
> 8 fresh dates
> ¼ pint (150 ml) natural yoghurt
> 1 clove garlic, crushed with a pinch sea salt
> ¼ tsp chilli powder
> 1½ oz (40 g) shelled walnuts, chopped

Take all the flesh from the mango shells and chop it. Divide it between 4 plates, piling it in the centre. Core the pineapple slices and cut each one into 8 pieces. Arrange them round the mango. Halve and stone the dates and place them between the pieces of pineapple.

Spoon the yoghurt over the mango and sprinkle it with a very little chilli powder.

Scatter the walnuts on top.

Melon, Coconut and Lime Salad

A pretty, soft green salad.

> 4 tbsp desiccated coconut
> juice 1 lime
> ¼ pint (150 ml) natural yoghurt
> ¼ tsp ground ginger
> pinch cayenne pepper
> 1 large honeydew melon
> 4 thin slices lime
> paprika

Mix together the coconut, lime juice, yoghurt, ginger and pepper. Leave for 1 hour so that the coconut becomes moist.

Cut the melon in half and remove the seeds. Scoop out the flesh in balls with a Parisienne scoop. Fold the melon balls into the coconut mixture and place in small bowls with a twist of lime on the top and a dusting of paprika.

Serve at once so that the juice does not have time to run from the melon and dilute the sauce.

Watermelon and Blackcurrant Salad

On a warm summer evening what could be better than this?

> 1 medium watermelon
> 4 oz (125 g) blackcurrants
> ¼ pint (150 ml) natural yoghurt
> 2 tbsp chopped mint
> 4 whole mint leaves

Quarter the watermelon. Scoop out and roughly chop the flesh, removing the seeds. String the blackcurrants.

Divide the melon between 4 small bowls. Spoon the yoghurt over the top. Scatter the mint leaves in the centre and the blackcurrants round the outside. Garnish each bowl with a whole mint leaf.

Red and Orange Nut Salad

12 oz (350 g) firm sweet tomatoes
2 small red peppers
1 large orange
4 tbsp olive oil, or walnut oil
2 tbsp white wine vinegar
1 clove garlic, crushed with a pinch sea salt
freshly ground black pepper
2 tbsp sesame seeds
1 oz (25 g) stoned dates, finely chopped
16 blanched almonds

Finely chop the tomatoes. Core, seed and finely chop the peppers. Cut the rind and pith from the orange and finely chop the flesh. Put them all into a bowl. Beat the oil, vinegar, garlic and pepper together and fold them into the salad.

Divide the salad between 4 small bowls. Put the sesame seeds into a frying pan and set them on a medium heat, stirring until they turn golden brown. Cool and scatter them over the salads with the dates.

Arrange 4 almonds in a star pattern on top of each salad.

Orange, Olive and Cheese Salad

4 large oranges
4 tbsp chopped chives
6 tbsp chopped parsley
12 black olives
4 oz (125 g) Mozzarella cheese

Cut the peel and pith from the oranges. Cut each orange into 6 thin slices. Arrange the slices on each of 4 small plates, making an overlapping circle and placing one in the centre. Scatter the chives and parsley over the top.

Halve and stone the olives. Put an olive half on to each orange slice. Cut the cheese into 20 small, even cubes or slices and arrange them round the edge.

Tomato and Egg Mayonnaise

1 small density or cos lettuce
12 oz (350 g) tomatoes
2 hard-boiled eggs
6 tbsp mayonnaise
1 tbsp tomato purée
1 tbsp chopped basil
1 tbsp chopped marjoram

Shred the lettuce and divide it between 4 small plates. Thinly slice the tomatoes and arrange them on top of the lettuce. Cut each egg in half. Remove and reserve the yolks and finely chop the whites.

Mix the egg whites into the mayonnaise with the tomato purée and herbs and spoon the mixture over the tomatoes. Rub the yolks through a sieve so they are scattered prettily over the top.

Little Anchovy Salads

1 bunch watercress
1 large orange
8 oz (225 g) firm tomatoes
16 green olives, stoned and quartered
4 tbsp chopped parsley
8 anchovy fillets
4 tbsp olive oil
2 tbsp white wine vinegar
1 clove garlic, crushed with a pinch sea salt
freshly ground black pepper

Chop the watercress. Cut the rind and pith from the orange. Cut the flesh into lengthways quarters and thinly slice it. Chop the tomatoes.

Arrange a bed of watercress on 4 small plates with the pieces of orange, tomato and olives on top. Scatter with parsley. Cut 4 of the anchovy fillets in half lengthways and arrange them in crosses on top of the salads.

Chop the remaining anchovies and pound them to a paste with a pestle and mortar. Work in the oil, vinegar, garlic and pepper and spoon the resulting dressing over the salads.

Smoked Mackerel on Cucumber

> 8 oz (225 g) smoked mackerel fillets
> 1 medium cucumber
> ¼ pint (150 ml) natural yoghurt
> 2 tbsp tomato purée
> 2 tbsp grated horseradish
> 2 tbsp chopped parsley

Flake the mackerel. Cut 24 ¼ inch (6 mm) thick rings from the cucumber and arrange 6 on each of 4 small plates.

Top each one with flaked mackerel. Beat the yoghurt, tomato purée and horseradish together and spoon them over the mackerel.

Scatter the parsley on top.

Tomatoes Stuffed with Fish and Cockles

> 8 oz (225 g) haddock or cod fillet
> 1 tbsp chopped lemon thyme
> juice 1½ lemons
> 8 large tomatoes
> 2 tbsp olive oil
> 1 tsp tomato purée
> 1 tbsp chopped fennel
> black pepper
> 4 oz (125 g) cockles

Skin the fish and cut it into small fillets. Scatter it with the lemon thyme and pour over the juice of ½ lemon. Leave the fish for 1 hour.

Preheat the oven to 350°F (180°C/gas 4). Place the fish on a lightly buttered heatproof plate. Cover with foil and bake for 20 minutes. Remove and allow to cool.

Scald and skin the tomatoes. Stand them stalk end down so they don't wobble around and cut off a little 'cap' from the top of each one. Scoop out all the seeds and inner flesh with a teaspoon and discard.

Combine the remaining lemon juice, the olive oil, tomato purée, fennel and black pepper. Flake the fish and mix it with the cockles and then thoroughly mix in the dressing. Stuff the tomatoes with the fish mixture and put back the caps at a jaunty angle.

Wholewheat Taramasalata

2 oz (50 g) wholewheat bread (weighed without crusts)
2 tbsp olive oil
4 oz (125 g) tinned cod's roe
1 tbsp grated onion
2 oz (50 g) fromage blanc
juice ½ lemon
2 tbsp tomato purée
pinch cayenne pepper
½ tsp ground paprika
4 black olives

Soak the bread in the oil for 5 minutes. Pound the cod's roe to a paste using a large pestle and mortar. Crumble the bread and add it to the roe. Pound together. Work in the grated onion and cheese. Add the lemon juice, tomato purée and cayenne pepper and keep pounding until you have a smooth, pale orange mixture.

Divide the taramasalata between 4 small plates. Sprinkle paprika in the centre. Halve and stone the olives and put them on top. Serve with plain, wholewheat biscuits or wholewheat pitta bread.

Fish Dishes

If the medieval law which imposed one 'fish day' on everyone per week (usually a Friday) and others on specific days in the year was to be reintroduced, it might well result in healthier eating habits. Fish is a nutritious, high protein food containing none of the saturated fats that have come to be so frowned upon. We ought to eat it at least once a week and preferably more.

White fish, in fact, contains only a trace of fat in the flaky flesh since all the oils are contained in the liver. It is an excellent source of iodine and contains some B vitamins. With oily fish, as the name implies, the fat is distributed throughout the body giving a much richer flavour and texture. It is a polyunsaturated fat and therefore will help to fight cholesterol levels, and it is high in vitamins A and D.

Forget the deep fried fish and chips. There are plenty of other ways of cooking fresh fish. You can bake, grill, steam, stir-fry or cook in a fish brick. One of my favourite ways of cooking white fish is to dice it, coat it in lemon juice and sprinkle it with herbs. Then I seal it in a parcel of lightly oiled or buttered foil, lay the parcel on a baking sheet and bake it in the oven. This seals in all the natural juices and flavour and keeps the fish moist. It is a particularly good way of cooking salmon steaks.

To bake white fish in a dish, sprinkle it with lemon or orange juice, a spice such as paprika or curry powder and some well-chosen herbs. Cover with lightly greased foil before baking it in a hot oven for 20 minutes.

Grill white fish in a dish: it is too flaky to stay together on a grill rack. Brush it lightly with oil and lemon juice first and if possible leave it to marinate for a few hours before cooking. Heat the grill to the highest temperature before putting the dish under the heat. Cook the fish on one side only until cooked through (when it no longer looks translucent).

For stir-frying, cut white fish into very small strips and cook them very quickly on a high heat. Long, slow frying will break the fish up.

Thick fish steaks, such as cod, or thick white fish fillets can be cooked in the oven in a fish brick. Lightly oil the inside of the brick first and rub it with a cut garlic clove. Lay a bed of herbs in the bottom half and put the fish on it. Cover with the other half of the brick and put into a preheated 450°F (230°C/gas 8) oven for 25 minutes. This is another way of sealing in all the natural juices, and the flavour of the herbs delicately penetrates right through. Remember, once you have used a brick for fish, keep it for fish as the flavour tends to stay.

Oily fish (herrings, mackerel, trout) can be cooked whole or filleted. They stand up well to grilling as their natural oils keep them moist. Whichever way you choose, use a perforated metal grill rack or, if you have only a wire type (like a cake cooling rack), cover it with foil pierced here and there with small holes. Get the rack and/or foil very hot with the grill at a high temperature before laying the fish on it. Otherwise the fish will curl up at the ends and you will never be able to flatten it again.

When grilling whole oily fish, it is a good idea to make slits in each side, running diagonally backwards and downwards from head to tail. This helps to distribute the heat and makes for even cooking. These slits can be filled with chopped herbs and brushed with oil and lemon juice which adds to both flavour and appearance.

Oily fish can also be baked in a packet, but it is best either kept whole or with the backbone removed and the fish reshaped. Put a sprig of herbs inside and wrap the fish individually in foil.

Sousing, baking fish in a water, wine or cider and vinegar mixture is a method which counteracts the richness of oily fish. Soused fish can be served hot or cold.

Fish can also be made into pâtés, casseroles and soups, so even if you ate fish every day you would still get plenty of variety.

Smoked Cod with Herb Vinaigrette

Fish doesn't have to be coated in, or floated on, rich sauces. A light, herby vinaigrette makes a superb summer meal.

> 2 lbs (900 g) smoked cod
> 1 bayleaf
> 1 tsp black peppercorns
> 1 blade mace
> 3 tbsp chopped parsley
> 3 tbsp chopped fennel
> 2 tbsp chopped chives
> 6 tbsp olive oil
> 3 tbsp white wine vinegar
> pinch cayenne pepper

Cut the cod into 4 serving pieces and put them into a wide-based saucepan with the bayleaf, peppercorns and mace. Cover with water and bring slowly to the boil. Simmer for 3 minutes. Lift out the fish, using a perforated fish slice so that it drains well. Place on a warm serving dish.

Put the remaining ingredients into a small saucepan and heat them to just below boiling point. Pour over the fish and serve.

Parcels of Haddock with Mustard

> 2 lbs (900 g) fresh haddock fillets
> 2 tsp mustard powder
> sea salt and freshly ground black pepper
> grated rind and juice 1 lemon
> 2 tbsp chopped parsley
> 4 spring onions, chopped
> butter for greasing

Preheat the oven to 400°F (200°C/gas 6). Skin the fillets and cut them into pieces about 1 × ½ inch (2.5 × 1.5 cm). Put them in a bowl and mix in the mustard powder, seasonings, lemon rind and juice, parsley and spring onions.

Butter 4 pieces of foil about 8 inch (20 cm) square and divide the fish between them. Seal the edges and place the parcels on a baking sheet. Bake in the oven for 20 minutes.

Take the parcels to the table and unwrap them on to individual plates.

Plaice with Lime and Fresh Coconut

You *must* use fresh coconut for this recipe; you need the liquid and desiccated coconut is too dry.

> 8 small plaice fillets
> grated rind and juice 2 limes
> ¼ tsp cayenne pepper
> ½ tsp ground ginger
> pinch sea salt
> 4 tbsp coconut liquid (from the middle of the coconut)
> 4 oz (125 g) freshly grated coconut

Put the plaice fillets into a large, flat, ovenproof dish, overlapping as little as possible (or use 2 dishes). Scatter them with the rind and juice of the limes, and with the pepper, ginger and a little salt. Allow to marinate for 4 hours at room temperature.

Preheat the oven to 400°F (200°/gas 6). Spoon the coconut liquid over the fish and scatter the grated coconut evenly over the top. Bake the fish, uncovered, for 15 minutes, so it is cooked through and the coconut is beginning to brown.

Pepper-topped Cod

> 2 lb (900 g) cod fillets
> juice 1 lemon
> 1 green pepper
> butter for greasing
> 1 tsp curry powder
> 2 tbsp chopped fresh coriander, or parsley

Skin the cod and cut it into ½ inch (1.5 cm) cubes. Put them on a plate, sprinkle with the lemon juice and leave for 30 minutes at room temperature.

Preheat the oven to 400°F (200°/gas 6). Core, seed and finely chop the pepper. Butter the dull side of 4 pieces of foil, each about 12 × 15 inches (30 × 37.5 cm).

Divide the cod between the pieces of foil. Sprinkle with the chopped pepper, curry powder and coriander. Bring the edges of the foil together and fold them over to seal them. Seal the ends and fold them upwards.

Lay the parcels of fish on a baking sheet and bake in the oven for 15 minutes. To serve, unwrap each parcel on to a separate dinner plate.

Hot Whiting Salad

Whiting cooks quickly, so it is an ideal fish for stir-frying. However, watch that you don't over-cook it, or it will break up. The salad will still taste good but won't look so appetizing.

> 4 small to medium whiting
> 8 oz (225 g) tomatoes
> 4 tbsp oil
> 1 large onion, quartered and thinly sliced
> 1 clove garlic, finely chopped
> 2 oz (50 g) sprouted alfalfa, or two boxes mustard
>   and cress
> juice 1 lemon

Fillet the whiting, skin the fillets if possible and cut them into ½ inch (1.5 cm) strips. Scald, skin and chop the tomatoes.

Heat the oil in a large frying pan over a high heat. Add the onion and garlic and cook them, stirring, for 2 minutes. Put in the whiting and cook in the same way for about 1 minute so it cooks through but doesn't break up. Mix in the tomatoes and alfalfa or mustard and cress and just heat them through. Pour in the lemon juice, let it bubble and serve immediately.

Skate with Tomato and Peanut Sauce

> 2 lbs (900 g) skate
> 1 lb (450 g) tomatoes
> 4 oz (125 g) unroasted peanuts
> 1 clove garlic, crushed with a pinch sea salt
> ¼ tsp Tabasco sauce
> 4 tbsp chopped parsley
>
> *Court bouillon*
> 4 tbsp dry white wine
> 1 medium onion, thinly sliced
> 1 large carrot, roughly chopped
> 1 celery stick, roughly chopped
> bouquet garni
> 1 tsp black peppercorns

Skin the skate if necessary and cut it into 8 even-sized pieces. Scald, skin and chop the tomatoes and put them into a blender or food processor. Add the peanuts, garlic, Tabasco sauce and chopped parsley and work everything to a purée. Put the purée into a saucepan and heat it, without boiling, over a low heat.

Put all the ingredients for the court bouillon into a large casserole adding enough water to cover the fish. Bring to the boil and simmer for 10 minutes. Put in the pieces of skate and poach them gently for 10 minutes. Remove and drain well.

Place the skate on a warm serving dish and spoon the tomato and peanut sauce over the top.

Grilled Bream with Avocados

Sea bream is a creamy textured fish so it goes excellently with both the flavour and texture of avocados.

> 1½ lbs (675 g) sea bream fillets
> grated rind and juice ½ medium orange
> 2 tbsp olive oil
> 1 tbsp tomato purée

few drops Tabasco sauce
1 small onion, finely chopped
1 clove garlic, crushed with a pinch sea salt
2 ripe avocados
2 tbsp chopped parsley

Skin the fillets and cut them into small serving pieces about 3 inches (8 cm) square. Mix the orange rind and juice, oil, tomato purée, Tabasco sauce, onion and garlic in a large, flat heatproof dish. Turn the pieces of fish in the mixture and leave them, cut side down, for at least 2 hours at room temperature.

Peel and stone the avocados. Cut them in half crossways and then into thin lengthways strips.

When you are ready to cook, heat the grill to high. Put the dish under the grill for 5 minutes. Turn the fish over and return the dish to the grill for 4 minutes. Scatter the avocado over the top and grill for 1 minute more. Serve straight from the dish.

Monkfish with Olives

Monkfish is a delicious fish with a texture somewhere between cod and mackerel.

1½ lb (675 g) monkfish fillets
10 green olives
grated rind and juice 1 lemon
6 tbsp dry white wine
1 clove garlic, crushed with a pinch sea salt
freshly ground black pepper
4 tbsp chopped parsley

Preheat the oven to 350°F (180°C/gas 4). Put the fillets into a flat, ovenproof dish. Stone and finely chop the olives. Mix them with the remaining ingredients. Spoon the olive mixture over the monkfish.

Cover the dish with foil and bake in the oven for 20 minutes or until the fish is cooked through.

Serve straight from the dish.

Herrings with Mustard Seeds

> 4 medium herrings
> 2 tsp mustard seeds
> juice 1 lemon
> 2 tbsp chopped lemon thyme or ordinary thyme
> freshly ground black pepper
> little oil for greasing

Preheat the oven to 400°F (200°C/gas 6). Head and gut the herrings and remove the backbones. Crush the mustard seeds coarsely. Lay the herrings out flat, cut side up, and sprinkle with the mustard seeds, lemon juice, lemon thyme and pepper. Reshape the herrings. Wrap each one in a piece of lightly oiled foil about 10 × 8 inches (25 × 20 cm) and lay the packets on a baking sheet.

Bake in the oven for 30 minutes. Unwrap on to individual plates to serve.

Parsley-coated Sardines

The lemon-flavoured parsley coating on these sardines keeps them moist so there is no need for any additional sauce or dressing.

> 1½–2 lbs (675–900 g) small sardines
> 2 oz (50 g) parsley
> 1 egg
> juice ½ lemon
> 2 oz (50 g) seasoned wholewheat flour

Clean the sardines but leave the heads on. Finely chop the parsley. Beat the egg with the lemon juice. Put the egg, parsley and flour on to 3 separate plates. Dip the sardines first in the egg, then touch both sides in the parsley and finally coat the whole fish in flour.

Heat the grill to high. Lay the sardines on the hot rack and grill them for 3 to 5 minutes on each side, depending on their size.

Serve them hot with a salad or a ratatouille of green peppers, courgettes and tomatoes.

Grilled Mackerel with Cloves and Apples

> 4 small to medium mackerel
> 4 tbsp cider vinegar
> 1 tsp ground cloves
> 4 small eating apples
> 4 tbsp olive oil

Fillet the mackerel and lay the fillets, not overlapping, in a large, flat dish. Sprinkle them with the vinegar and half the cloves. Core the apples and cut them into thin slices. In a bowl, mix the remaining ground cloves with the oil and fold in the apples. Leave the mackerel and apples for 30 minutes.

Preheat the grill to high. (If you have an open wire rack, cover it with foil.) Lay the slices of mackerel, skin side down, on the hot rack and grill for 4 minutes. Lay the apple rings on top and grill them for another 2 minutes.

Serve with jacket potatoes, lightly cooked vegetables or a salad.

Finnish Mackerel Hotpot

> 4 medium mackerel
> 2 lb (900 g) potatoes
> 4 allspice berries, crushed
> freshly ground black pepper
> grated rind ½ lemon
> ¼ pint (150 ml) stabilized yoghurt (see page 13)
> 4 tbsp chopped parsley

Fillet the mackerel and cut into 1 inch (2.5 cm) pieces. Scrub the potatoes and cut them into ½ inch (1.5 cm) dice. Put the potatoes into a saucepan with the allspice, pepper, lemon rind and 1 pint of water. Bring to the boil and simmer for 20 minutes or until soft. Add the mackerel and simmer for a further 5 minutes until it is cooked through. Mix in the yoghurt and reheat if necessary.

Turn out into a serving dish and scatter the parsley over the top.

Marinated Mackerel Pâté

> 1 small onion
> 1 clove garlic
> grated rind and juice ½ lemon
> 2 tbsp olive oil
> few sprigs thyme
> black pepper
> 2 medium mackerel, filleted
> 8 oz (225 g) smoked mackerel fillet
> 1 tbsp grated horseradish
> 1 tbsp chopped capers

Finely chop the onion and garlic and mix them with the lemon rind and juice and the olive oil. Put the mixture into a large flat dish. Scatter with the thyme and pepper.

Bury the pieces of mackerel and smoked mackerel, cut side down, in the marinade, making sure some of the pieces of onion cover the skin side. Leave to marinate for about 4 hours.

Preheat the grill to high. Lay the mackerel pieces, skin side down, on the hot rack or foil (make sure a few pieces of onion and garlic are still clinging to them). Cook the fish until they begin to turn golden.

Allow to cool slightly and then pound the fish with a large pestle and mortar, or in a bowl with a wooden spoon. Work in the capers and horseradish. Pack the mixture into an oiled dish or mould. Cover and chill until firm.

Serve with a salad.

Soused Trout

4 medium trout
3 tbsp white wine vinegar
6 tbsp dry white wine
4 tbsp mixed chopped parsley, lemon thyme
   and marjoram
freshly ground black pepper
16 almonds (optional) to garnish

Preheat the oven to 350°F (180°C/gas 4). Fillet the trout and cut each fillet in half. Lay the pieces in a large, flat, ovenproof dish. Pour the wine vinegar and wine over them, sprinkle with the herbs and grind over some pepper. Cover the dish completely with foil and put it into the oven for 30 minutes.

Leave the dish in a cool place, still covered, until the trout is cold. It can easily be left overnight.

Serve straight from the dish putting an almond on each piece of trout.

Grilled Minted Trout

4 medium trout
6 tbsp olive oil
juice 1 lemon
½ tsp ground coriander
sea salt and freshly ground black pepper
6 tbsp chopped mint

Clean the trout and cut the tails into V-shapes. Remove the heads if you wish. Cut three diagonal slits on each side, sloping backwards from head to tail.

Beat together the oil, lemon juice, coriander and seasonings. Brush the trout with the mixture, inside and out and also in the slits. Press chopped mint into the slits. Place the trout in a dish and pour over any remaining oil mixture. Leave for at least 4 hours at room temperature.

When you are ready to cook, heat the grill to high. (If you have an open wire rack, cover it with foil.) Lay the fish on the hot rack and grill them so they are browned on each side and cooked through – about 10 minutes altogether.

Herbed Salmon

Salmon must be cooked lightly and simply to preserve all the juices and flavour. Foil packets seal them both in.

> 4 large salmon steaks
> freshly ground black pepper
> juice ½ lemon
> 1 tbsp chopped lemon thyme
> 2 tbsp chopped marjoram
> 4 sorrel leaves, chopped
> ½ oz (15 g) unsalted butter

Preheat the oven to 400°F (200°C/gas 6). Skin the salmon steaks and remove as many bones as possible. Put each one on a piece of buttered foil about 10 inches (25 cm) square. Grind over the pepper, squeeze over a little lemon juice, scatter with the herbs and dot with a small knob of butter. Seal the foil over the salmon and turn up the ends so the juices cannot run out.

Place the packets on a baking sheet and bake in the oven for 20 minutes. Unwrap the packets on to individual dinner plates to preserve all the juices.

Seafood Gumbo

A gumbo is a Creole dish containing okra, which acts as a thickener.

> 2 medium whiting
> juice ½ lemon
> salt and freshly ground black pepper
> 8 oz (225 g) prawns, weighed in their shells
> 1 medium crab
> 8 oz (225 g) tomatoes
> 3 tbsp oil

1 lb (450 g) okra
2 medium onions, finely chopped
1 clove garlic, finely chopped
1 tsp paprika
¼ tsp cayenne pepper
1 pint (575 ml) fish stock (made from whiting
trimmings and prawn shells)
1 tsp Tabasco sauce

Fillet the whiting. Lay the fillets in a flat dish and sprinkle them with the lemon juice and pepper. Leave them for at least 1 hour and then cut them into ½ inch (1.5 cm) strips.

Shell the prawns. Make a stock using the prawn shells and whiting trimmings. Take all the meat from the crab. Scald, skin and chop the tomatoes.

Heat the oil in a large saucepan over a low heat. Stir in the okra, onions and garlic and cook until soft. Stir in the paprika, cayenne pepper and tomatoes. Pour in the fish stock and bring it to the boil. Add the whiting. Cover and simmer for 1 hour. Stir in the prawns, crab meat and Tabasco sauce and reheat if necessary.

Serve in soup bowls with wholewheat bread or cornbread, or in large bowls poured over plainly cooked brown rice.

Meat Dishes

Provided that you don't eat meat every day and that you buy good quality lean meat and cook it without added fat, it can still be part of a healthy diet. It is best not to eat meat twice a day and probably not more than four times a week and you should eat it with vegetables, pulses or grains. Now for the good news. Meat is a good source of B vitamins, especially $B12$ which is found in few other foods. Red meats and offal are rich in iron and the lighter meats are a good source of potassium. Meat is a high protein food but unfortunately it does contain saturated fats, not only round the edge but also in the muscle fibres. So, in order to cut down on the fat as much as possible, buy the leanest meat that you can find and use little or no fat when cooking.

Grilling is a simple way of cooking meat that allows the fat to drip away. Only the best quality meats are suitable for grilling. They can be marinated first in wine or lemon and orange juice plus some chopped herbs, or they can simply be placed on the hot grill rack and spread with mustard or sprinkled with herbs. Beef, in the form of steak, should be brushed very lightly with a little oil before grilling. Pork and lamb are so rich that you need not do this. Beefburgers (make them yourself from best quality mince) contain some fat and should not be basted. Liver and kidneys need basting or marinating.

When roasting meat, there is absolutely no need to spread it liberally with butter or dripping before it goes into the oven. Place it on a rack in a roasting tin and put it straight into the oven. All the fat will drip away into the tin and your joint will be none the worse for it. When cooking lamb and pork, lay sprigs of herbs such as rosemary, thyme or sage above and below the meat and insert thin slivers of garlic into narrow slits cut with a small sharp knife. Beef can be rubbed with mustard powder and sprinkled occasionally with wholewheat flour.

Another way of cooking whole joints of meat is to pot-roast them. Put them into a casserole with a very little liquid (¼ pint/150 ml will be plenty), such as wine, cider or orange juice. Add some vegetables for flavour, cover and bake in the oven.

The conventional method of braising or casseroling meat is to brown it first, remove it from the pan and use the same fat to soften the onions and other vegetables. Then add liquid, replace the meat and put it in the oven. This browning process definitely produces a richer flavoured casserole than one in which the vegetables and meat are simply covered with liquid, brought to the boil and put into the oven – but you do have the added fat. I have discovered a way of having the advantage of both methods. Instead of fat use ¼ pint (150 ml) stock. Bring it to the boil in your casserole, add the onion (nearly always an essential ingredient) and boil until the onion is soft and all but about 2 tbsp of the stock have evaporated, leaving a syrupy glaze. Add the meat and stir it about until it browns – it will, don't worry. Remove the meat and stir in any other vegetables in the recipe. Then pour in the liquid, bring it to the boil and replace the meat. This makes a rich casserole very close in flavour to the one made by using the conventional browning method. Any casserole or braising recipe can be adapted to this method.

Another step towards healthy eating is to replace some of the meat in a casserole with extra vegetables or soaked pulses (beans and lentils). These casseroles are extremely tasty since the added ingredients will thicken and enrich the casserole juices while themselves picking up the flavour of the meat, liquids and herbs.

The Chinese have many recipes for steaming meat but they insist that only the best quality meats should be used. Battery-reared chickens, for example, are supposed to taste of the fish meal on which they were fed. So you should buy a genuine free-range chicken, before trying the steamed chicken recipe on page 73.

Try to have a variety of different types of meat each week so that you obtain the widest possible range of nutrients. Don't forget about iron-rich offal, and why not try some game for a change? It is the most widely available free-range meat and, in the height of the season, pheasant in particular is not as expensive as you might think. Wood pigeons are available all the year round from good supermarkets at a very reasonable price.

The following recipes should give you an idea of how interesting low fat or no-fat cooking can be.

Quick Curry-burgers

Yoghurt gives beefburgers a light, fresh flavour.

>   1½ lbs (675 g) minced beef
>   4 fl oz (125 ml) natural yoghurt
>   1 clove garlic, crushed with a pinch sea salt
>   1 tsp curry paste

Put the beef into a mixing bowl. Beat the yoghurt with the garlic and curry paste until the mixture is smooth. Beat it into the minced beef. Form the beef into 8 small, round burger shapes. Chill for 30 minutes so they set into shape.

Preheat the grill to high. (If you have an open wire rack, cover it with foil.) Lay the burgers on the hot rack and grill them, turning them once, so they are brown on both sides – about 8 minutes.

Beef in a Packet with Mushrooms

>   1½ lbs (675 g) beef skirt
>   8 oz (225 g) open mushrooms
>   2 tbsp chopped parsley
>   1 tbsp chopped thyme
>   1 clove garlic, very finely chopped
>   2 tbsp Worcestershire sauce
>   butter for greasing

Preheat the oven to 400°F (200°C/gas 6). Cut the beef into very small, thin slivers. Halve the mushrooms if they are large and thinly slice them. Put the beef and mushrooms into a bowl and fold in the herbs, garlic and Worcestershire sauce. Divide the mixture between 4 pieces of buttered foil 12 × 16 inches (30 × 40 cm). Bring two sides of the foil together and fold them over. Seal the ends and fold them upwards. Cook for 1 hour.

Transfer the contents of each parcel to individual dinner plates to serve.

Braised Beef with Grated Carrot

The grated carrots in this casserole soften and act as a thickener to the liquid. If sherry is not available, use red wine or beer, white wine with the addition of 1 tbsp tomato purée, or simply use extra stock.

> 1 lb (450 g) braising steak or beef skirt
> 8 oz (225 g) leeks
> 1 lb (450 g) carrots
> ¾ pint (425 ml) stock
> 1 tbsp chopped parsley
> 1 tbsp chopped savory
> ¼ pint (150 ml) dry sherry (see above)

Preheat the oven to 350°F (180°C/gas 4). Cut the beef into ¾ inch (2 cm) dice. Thinly slice the leeks. Grate the carrots.

Bring half the stock to the boil in a flameproof casserole dish. Add the leeks and cook them, uncovered, until they are soft and all but about 1 tbsp of the stock has evaporated. Remove the leeks. Add the pieces of beef and brown them quickly, stirring. Pour in the remaining stock and bring it to the boil. Add the carrots, leeks and herbs and pour in the sherry.

Cover the casserole and cook it in the oven for 1¼ hours.

Beef Pot-roasted with Orange

Beef, tenderized and flavoured with orange – this is a light and low fat way to pot-roast.

> grated rind and juice 2 large oranges
> ¼ tsp cayenne pepper
> 1 large onion, finely chopped
> 4 tbsp chopped parsley
> 1 clove garlic, crushed with a pinch sea salt
> 2½–3 lb (1–1.25 kg) topside of beef, in one piece.

In a casserole, mix together the orange rind and juice, cayenne pepper, onion, parsley and garlic. Turn the meat in the mixture and leave it to marinate, covered, for 6 to 8 hours at room temperature.

Preheat the oven to 350°F (180°C/gas 4). Cook the casserole for 2 hours.

Carve the meat and serve with any juices from the casserole dish spooned over the top.

Hot Beef and Pinto Beans

This is a warming spicy stew, good on a winter's night. Brown kidney beans can be used if pinto beans are not available.

> 8 oz (225 g) pinto beans
> 1 lb (450 g) stewing beef
> 2 large onions
> 2 large carrots
> 4 celery sticks
> ¾ pint (425 ml) tomato juice
> ¼ pint (150 ml) stock
> 1 clove garlic, crushed with a pinch sea salt
> 2 tsp paprika
> ¼ tsp cayenne pepper
> bouquet garni

Put the pinto beans into a saucepan and cover them with water. Bring to the boil, boil for 10 minutes and remove them from the heat. Leave to soak for 2 hours. Drain.

Preheat the oven to 325°F (170°C/gas 3). Trim the beef of any fat and cut it into ¾ inch (2 cm) cubes. Thinly slice the onions and carrots and chop the celery. Mix the beans, beef and vegetables in a flameproof casserole dish. Pour in the tomato juice and stock and add the garlic, paprika, cayenne pepper and bouquet garni. Bring to the boil over a moderate heat. Cover the casserole and cook it in the oven for 2 hours or until both beef and beans are tender.

Serve with plainly cooked brown rice or jacket potatoes.

Veal Escalopes in Light Cheese Sauce

Curd cheese makes a rich tasting but low caloried sauce.

    4 veal escalopes
    2 tbsp olive oil
    freshly ground black pepper
    ½ pint (275 ml) stock
    1 medium onion, finely chopped
    grated rind and juice ½ lemon
    2 tbsp chopped parsley
    2 tbsp chopped thyme
    2 oz (50 g) curd cheese

Heat the grill to the highest temperature. Brush the veal escalopes with the oil and season them with the pepper. Pour 4 fl oz (125 ml) of the stock into a frying pan and bring it to the boil. Add the onion and simmer it, uncovered, until all the stock has evaporated. Meanwhile grill the escalopes for 2 minutes on each side.

Pour the remaining stock into the frying pan and bring it to the boil. Add the lemon rind and juice, herbs and escalopes. Cover and simmer for 20 minutes.

Take the pan from the heat. Place the escalopes on a warm serving dish. Stir the cheese into the liquid in the pan, making sure it is smoothly blended. Spoon the sauce over the escalopes and serve.

Simple Pork and Leeks

    1½ lbs (675 g) lean, boneless pork, from spare rib
        chops, shoulder or the lean end of the belly
    12 oz (350 g) leeks
    2 tsp mustard powder
    8 sage leaves, chopped
    sea salt and freshly ground black pepper
    2 tbsp dry white wine or cider
    little butter or oil for greasing

Preheat the oven to 400°F (200°C/gas 6). Cut the pork into ⅜ inch (1 cm) dice. Trim, wash and thinly slice the leeks. Put the pork and leeks into a bowl and mix in the mustard, sage, seasonings and wine or cider. Lightly grease the dull side of 4 pieces of foil 12 by 16 inches (30 × 40 cm). Divide the pork between them. Bring up the sides of the foil and fold them over several times. Fold the ends upwards.

Lay the packets on a baking sheet and bake them in the oven for 1 hour.

Empty the parcels on to individual plates to serve.

Pork, Cabbage and Apple Casserole

Pork, cabbage, apples and cider have been served together for many years in many different countries, and are one of the most satisfying combinations of ingredients. They make a lovely light, casserole dish. A tomato salad would be a good accompaniment or some lightly cooked carrots.

> 1¼ lbs (575 g) lean boneless pork
> 4 oz (125 g) bacon
> 1 large green cabbage
> 1 large cooking apple
> 1 medium onion
> ¼ pint (150 ml) dry cider
> little freshly ground nutmeg
> ½ tsp ground cinnamon

Preheat the oven to 350°F (180°C/gas 4). Cut the pork into ¾ inch (2 cm) dice. Chop the bacon. Finely shred the cabbage. Peel, core and slice the apple and thinly slice the onion.

Put the bacon into a flameproof casserole dish and set it on a low heat. Leave it until it is cooked through but not brown and there is enough fat in the pan to cook the pork. Take out the bacon and raise the heat. Add the pork and brown it, stirring it all the time to drive away any moisture that may collect. (If your casserole has a small base, do this in two batches.) Remove the pork and lower the heat.

Stir in the cabbage, apple and onion. Pour in the cider and

bring it to the boil. Mix in the spices and replace the pork and bacon. Cover the casserole and cook in the oven for 1 hour.

Barbequed Pork in a Brick

Cooking pork in a brick ensures that the barbeque flavour penetrates right through it. However, if you don't have a brick, the pork can be roasted in the usual way.

> 2½–3 lb (1–1.25 kg) joint shoulder of pork
> 2 tbsp tamari sauce
> 1 tbsp tomato purée
> 1 tbsp honey
> 2 tbsp cider vinegar
> 1 clove garlic, crushed with a pinch sea salt

Preheat the oven to 450°F (230°C/gas 8). Cut the rind from the pork. Mix together the remaining ingredients. Place the pork in the brick and spoon the barbeque mixture over it, making sure all surfaces are coated.

Put on the lid and bake in the oven for 2 hours. The meat will be very dark in colour after cooking because of the effect of the honey. It won't be burned or spoiled as it really does need this longer cooking time.

Pork Grill with Orange Mustard

Spare-rib chops are small and oblong with only a tiny piece of fat at one end.

> 1 lb (450 g) spare rib chops
> 12 oz (350 g) pig's liver
> 2 tbsp mustard powder
> grated rind and juice 1 large orange
> 2 tsp chopped rosemary
> 6 sage leaves, chopped

Cut the chops into pieces about 2 inches (5 cm) square. Trim away some of the fat, cut it into thin strips and reserve it. Cut the liver into fairly thick pieces. Put the mustard powder into a bowl with the orange rind and gradually mix in the orange juice. Mix in the herbs. Spread the mustard mixture over the pieces of pork and liver and leave them at room temperature for 1 hour.

When you are ready to cook, heat the grill to high. Lay the pieces of pork and liver on the hot rack and place strips of the pork fat over the liver to baste it. Cook until the chops are brown (about 8 minutes). Turn over the chops and liver and brown the other side. Discard the pieces of fat. Serve the meats quite plainly. Cabbage is a good accompaniment.

Alternative: one pig's kidney, cut in half lengthways and then in half again crossways, can be added to the meats.

Ham Risotto

8 oz (225 g) lean cooked ham
1 medium aubergine
2 large green peppers
4 tbsp olive oil
1 large onion, finely chopped
1 clove garlic, finely chopped
8 oz (225 g) short grain brown rice
1½ pints (850 ml) chicken stock
1 tbsp tomato purée
freshly ground black pepper
4 oz (125 g) Gruyère or Emmental cheese, grated

Cut both ham and aubergines into ½ inch (1.5 cm) dice. Core, seed and finely chop the peppers.

Heat the oil in a heavy saucepan over a low heat. Add the onion and garlic and soften them. Stir in the rice, aubergine and peppers and cook, stirring, for 2 minutes. Pour in ½ pint (275 ml) of the stock and bring it to the boil. Cook, uncovered, over a low heat until most of the stock has been absorbed, about 10 minutes. Stir in the remaining stock and bring to the boil. Add the tomato purée and season with the pepper. Mix in the ham.

Cook gently, uncovered, stirring frequently, until almost all the stock has been absorbed. This will take about 45 minutes. Take the pan from the heat and fork in the cheese.

Lamb Chops with Summer Herbs

Vinegar and fresh herbs make a piquant sauce for lamb chops. Serve with new potatoes and a selection of summer vegetables.

> 4 good-sized loin chops
> 2 tbsp chopped parsley
> 1 tbsp chopped mint
> 1 tbsp chopped marjoram
> 1 tbsp chopped thyme
> 1 sorrel leaf, finely chopped
> 4 tbsp red wine vinegar
> 4 tbsp stock

Preheat the oven to 350°F (180°C/gas 4). Place the chops in a casserole dish and cover them with the herbs. Spoon in the vinegar and stock and cook in the oven for 1¼ hours.

Lamb with Lemon and Tarragon

A brightly coloured vegetable such as carrots, peas or spinach goes best with this.

> 1½ lb (675 g) lean boneless lamb cut from the shoulder
>   or leg
> ¼ pint (150 ml) stock
> 1 large onion, thinly sliced
> ¼ pint (150 ml) stabilized yoghurt (see page 13)
> juice 1 lemon
> 2 tbsp chopped tarragon, or 2 tsp dried
> 1 clove garlic, crushed with a pinch sea salt
> freshly ground black pepper

Cut the lamb into 1 inch (2.5 cm) cubes. Bring the stock to the boil in a large casserole dish over a high heat. Add the onion and cook it over a medium heat until it is soft and the stock has reduced by about three-quarters. Raise the heat. Add the lamb and stir it around to sear it. Then add the yoghurt, lemon juice, tarragon, garlic and pepper.

Cover the casserole and leave it on a low heat for about 1 hour, or until the lamb is tender.

Far Eastern Breast of Lamb

If you thought breast of lamb was fatty and inedible, try cooking it by this method.

> 2 lbs (900 g) breast of lamb
>
> *Marinade*
> 2 tbsp sesame oil
> 2 tbsp tamari sauce
> 2 tbsp tomato purée
> juice 1 lemon or lime
> 1 clove garlic, crushed with a pinch sesame salt,
>   or sea salt
> ¼ tsp cayenne pepper

Cut the breast of lamb into pieces about 1 × 4 inches (2.5 × 10 cm). In a large flat dish, mix together all the ingredients for the marinade. Turn the pieces of lamb in the marinade and leave them to stand for 6 to 8 hours at room temperature.

Preheat the oven to 400°F (200°C/gas 6). Put the pieces of lamb on a rack in a roasting tin and cook in the oven for 45 minutes until they are browned and crisp.

Serve with brown rice.

Curried Lamb Pilaf

The amounts of spices given here make a mild flavoured curry. Extra chilli powder can be added if you wish to make it stronger.

> 1 lb (450 g) lean, boneless lamb cut from the shoulder
>   or leg
> 1 lb (450 g) carrots

1 lb (450 g) peas (weighed before shelling),
  or 8 oz (225 g) frozen peas
12 oz (350 g) potatoes
1 green pepper
1 pint (575 ml) stock
1 large onion, finely chopped
1 clove garlic, finely chopped
1 tsp garam masala
½ tsp ground ginger
¼ tsp chilli powder (see above)
8 oz (225 g) long grain brown rice

Cut the lamb into ¾ inch (2 cm) cubes. Slice the carrots, shell the peas, scrub and dice the potatoes and core and seed the pepper and cut it into 1 inch (2.5 cm) strips.

Put ¼ pint (150 ml) of the stock into a large, flameproof casserole dish and bring it to the boil. Add the onion and garlic and cook until all but 2 tbsp of the stock has evaporated. Add the meat and stir until it browns. Stir in the spices and then the vegetables. Pour in the remaining stock and bring to the boil. Cover and simmer for 1 hour.

Meanwhile, boil the rice in lightly salted water for 20 minutes. Drain it and rinse with cold water. Add it to the casserole and continue cooking for a further 20 to 25 minutes or until the rice is tender and all the stock has been absorbed.

Yoghurt Kibbeh

This is a lamb and wheat 'cake' that is surprisingly moist and light and almost creamy in texture.

8oz (225 g) burghul wheat (see page 125)
1 lb (450 g) lean, boneless lamb cut from the shoulder
  or leg
1 small onion, grated
1 clove garlic, crushed with a pinch sea salt
1 oz (25 g) parsley, finely chopped
1 tbsp tomato purée
½ tsp ground ginger
¼ tsp ground cinnamon

¼ tsp cayenne pepper
¼ pint (150 ml) natural yoghurt
1 oz (25 g) pine kernels
oil for greasing

Preheat the oven to 350°F (180°C/gas 4). Soak the wheat in warm water for 30 minutes. Drain and squeeze it dry.

Finely mince the lamb twice. Add the onion, garlic, parsley, tomato purée, spices and yoghurt and mix well. Divide the mixture into two. Mix one half with the burghul wheat. Finely grind the pine kernels and add them to the other half.

Oil an 8 inch (20 cm) diameter cake tin. Put in half the lamb and burghul wheat mixture, then all the lamb and pine kernel mixture and smooth it out in an even layer. Top with the remaining lamb and burghul wheat.

Bake the kibbeh for 45 minutes or until the top is golden brown. Serve it hot with a salad.

Simply Grilled Chicken Livers with Thyme

This simple way of cooking chicken livers flavours them well and ensures they are soft and melting in texture. If you haven't much time, you can leave them in the marinade for only 10 minutes and still achieve delicious results.

1½ lb (675 g) chicken livers
4 tbsp chopped thyme
4 tbsp olive oil
3 tbsp dry red wine
1 clove garlic, crushed with a pinch sea salt
freshly ground black pepper

Trim the chicken livers. Mix the remaining ingredients together in a large bowl. Fold in the livers and leave them for 2 hours at room temperature.

When you are ready to cook, preheat the grill to high. (If you have an open wire rack, cover it with foil.) Place the livers on the hot rack and grill them on one side only (the heat from the rack will cook the other side) for about 4 minutes so they are firm and lightly browned but still pink in the centre.

Serve with the juices from the grill pan spooned over them.

Lamb's Liver with Peppers and Tomatoes

This rich, but fat-free, liver dish is easy to make and good enough for guests.

>   1½ lb (675 g) lamb's liver
>   2 red peppers
>   2 green peppers
>   1 lb (450 g) tomatoes
>   1 medium onion
>   ½ pint (275 ml) stock
>   1 clove garlic, finely chopped
>   1 tbsp chopped thyme

Cut the lamb's liver into small, thin slivers. Core and seed the peppers and cut them into 1 inch (2.5 cm) strips. Scald, skin and chop the tomatoes. Finely chop the onion.

Pour the stock into a frying pan and bring it to the boil over a high heat. Add the peppers, onion and garlic and cook over a medium heat until the onion is soft and nearly all the stock has evaporated. Add the tomatoes and thyme and cook until the tomatoes are bubbling. Add the liver. Cook for 3 minutes or until the liver is cooked through but still soft.

Herbed Chicken with Nut Topping

>   3 lb (1.25 kg) roasting chicken
>   4 tbsp olive oil
>   juice 1 lemon
>   6 tbsp mixed chopped parsley, thyme, marjoram
>   and sage
>   1 medium onion, finely chopped
>   1½ oz (40 g) shelled walnuts
>   1½ oz (40 g) shelled hazelnuts

Cut the chicken into 8 serving pieces. In a dish, mix together the oil, lemon juice, herbs and onion. Turn the chicken in the mixture and leave it, covered, for 12 hours at room temperature.

When you are ready to cook, preheat the oven to 400°F (200°C/gas 6). Drain the chicken pieces and reserve the marinade. Put the chicken pieces, attractively arranged and skin side up, into a shallow, oven-to-table dish. Cook in the oven for 30 minutes.

While the chicken is cooking, grind or very finely chop the nuts and mix them to a paste with the remaining marinade. Spread the paste over the chicken pieces and return to the oven for a further 15 minutes.

Either serve straight from the oven, or serve cold with a salad.

Chicken Steamed with Tamari

For this recipe, choose a free-range chicken for the best possible flavour.

> 3–3½ lb (1.25–1.6 kg) chicken (see above)
> 1 medium onion, finely chopped
> 4 tbsp chopped parsley
> 2 tbsp tamari sauce
> 1 tbsp sesame oil
> ½ tsp mustard powder

Cut the chicken into 4 serving pieces. Mix the remaining ingredients together. Put each piece of chicken on a piece of foil about 12 inches (30 cm) square and spoon the onion mixture over the top.

Seal the edges of the foil well and lay the parcels of chicken in a large open steamer. Set them over a pan of simmering water, cover and cook for 1½ hours.

Unwrap the packets on to the individual dinner plates to preserve all the juices.

Nourishing Chicken Broth

This is an excellent way of making one chicken serve 6 people.

> 3–3½ lb (1.25–1.6 kg) roasting chicken
> bouquet garni
> sea salt and freshly ground black pepper
> 2 oz (50 g) brown rice
> 2 medium potatoes, finely diced
> 2 large carrots, finely diced
> 2 large celery sticks, finely diced
> 1 large onion, finely diced
> 2 leeks, finely diced
> 8 oz (225 g) pumpkin or swede, finely diced

Put the chicken into a large casserole dish (about 10 pints/5.75 l if possible) and cover it with water. Add the bouquet garni and season well. Bring to the boil, and skim if necessary. Cover and simmer for 15 minutes. Add the rice and simmer for a further 45 minutes. Then add the vegetables and continue cooking for a further 30 minutes.

Take the pan from the heat and remove the chicken. Cut all the meat from the bones and dice it finely. Return it to the soup. Remove the bouquet garni and reheat if necessary.

Serve the soup in big deep bowls, accompanied by wholewheat bread.

Middle Eastern Chicken Salad

> 3½ lb (1.6 kg) roasting chicken
> ½ lemon, thinly sliced
> 1 tsp ground cinnamon
> 1 tsp ground ginger
>
> *Boiling*
> 1 small onion, halved
> 1 medium carrot, roughly chopped
> 1 medium celery stick, roughly chopped

bouquet garni
1 tsp black peppercorns

Salad
¼ pint (150 ml) natural yoghurt
½ tsp ground cinnamon
½ tsp ground ginger
3 oz (75 g) stoned dates, chopped
8 oz (225 g) burghul wheat (see page 125)
4 tbsp olive oil
juice ½ lemon
1 clove garlic, crushed with a pinch sea salt
3 tbsp chopped parsley
freshly ground black pepper
½ lemon, thinly sliced

Truss the chicken, putting the lemon inside. Mix together the cinnamon and ginger and rub into the chicken skin. Put the chicken into a saucepan with the boiling ingredients and pour in water to just above the legs. Bring to the boil, cover and simmer for 50 minutes or until the chicken is tender. Remove the chicken and allow to cool.

Cut all the meat from the bones and dice it. Mix the yoghurt with the spices and fold it into the chicken. Add the dates.

Soak the burghul wheat in warm water for 30 minutes. Drain and squeeze it dry. Beat together the oil, lemon juice and garlic and mix them into the wheat with the parsley. Season with the pepper.

Put a ring of the wheat on a large flat serving dish. Pile the chicken salad in the centre and garnish with the lemon slices.

Turkey with Apricot and Nut Stuffing

This is a real treat for Christmas

12–14 lb (5.5–6.5 kg) turkey

Stuffing
4 oz (125 g) dried apricots
½ pint (275 ml) dry white wine

3 oz (75 g) shelled walnuts
3 oz (75 g) shelled hazelnuts
1 oz (25 g) butter
2 large onions, thinly sliced
8 oz (225 g) fresh wholewheat breadcrumbs
2 tbsp chopped thyme
2 tbsp chopped marjoram
1 tbsp chopped savory
2 tsp chopped sage
sea salt and freshly ground black pepper
¼ tsp ground mace

Gravy
½ pint (275 ml) stock, made from the giblets
¼ pint (150 ml) dry white wine

For the stuffing, soak the apricots in half the wine for 6 hours. Drain and finely chop them. Measure the liquid that is left and make it up to ¼ pint (150 ml) with more wine. Grind the nuts or chop them very finely.

Melt the butter in a large frying pan over a low heat. Add the onions and soften them. Take the pan from the heat and mix in the breadcrumbs, nuts, herbs, seasonings and mace. Bind the mixture with the apricot juices and wine.

Preheat the oven to 400°F (200°C/gas 6). Stuff and truss the turkey. Put the turkey on a rack in a roasting tin and cover it completely with foil. Cook in the oven for 2 hours. There is no need to baste it as the foil will keep it moist. Remove the foil and put the turkey back into the oven for a further 30 minutes to brown.

Lift the turkey on to a large serving dish. Remove the rack from the pan. Spoon off any excess fat. Set the pan on top of the stove over a high heat. Pour in the stock and wine and bring them to the boil, stirring in any residue from the bottom of the pan. Simmer the gravy for 5 minutes, pour it into a warmed sauce boat and serve with the turkey.

Duck with Pineapple and Green Peppers

Serve this Chinese-flavoured duck with plainly cooked brown rice.

  4 lb (1.8 kg) duck
  1 tsp sea salt
  12 thick slices fresh pineapple, cored
  1 large green pepper
  1 large onion, thinly sliced
  1 clove garlic, finely chopped
  4 tbsp sugar-free marmalade
  ½ pint (275 ml) stock
  2 tbsp tamari sauce

Preheat the oven to 400°F (200°C/gas 6). Prick the duck all over with a fork and rub the salt into the skin. Put the duck on a rack in a roasting tin and cover it with foil. Cook in the oven for 1¼ hours.

Cut each pineapple slice in half. Core and seed the pepper and cut it into 1 × ¼ inch (2.5 cm × 6 mm) pieces. Thinly slice the onion. Put the pepper, onion and garlic in the bottom of an oven-to-table dish, about 2 inches (5 cm) deep.

Take the duck from the oven. Allow it to cool slightly and cut it into four joints. Put the joints on top of the pepper and onion. Spread each joint with 1 tbsp marmalade. Pour the excess fat from the roasting tin. Set the tin over a high heat. Pour in the stock and bring it to the boil, stirring in any residue from the bottom of the pan. Simmer this gravy for 2 minutes. Add the tamari sauce and then pour the gravy over the duck. Put a piece of pineapple on each duck joint.

Put the duck back into the oven for a further 30 minutes. Serve straight from the dish.

A Simple Casserole of Pigeons

    4 wood pigeons
    4 rashers unsmoked streaky bacon
    8 oz (225 g) carrots
    8 oz (225 g) mushrooms
    1 large onion, thinly sliced
    3 tbsp chopped parsley
    freshly ground black pepper
    ¾ pint (425 ml) stock

Preheat the oven to 300°F (160°C/gas 2). Truss the pigeons. Cut the bacon rashers into 2 or 3 pieces depending on their size and lay them over the breasts of the pigeons.

Thinly slice the carrots and mushrooms. Put them into a wide-based casserole dish and mix in the onion and parsley. Season with plenty of freshly ground black pepper. Bury the pigeons in the vegetables with the bacon over the top just showing. Pour in the stock.

Cover the casserole and cook in the oven for 2½ hours. Serve the pigeons surrounded by the vegetables.

Poached Pheasant with Celery

Poaching a pheasant might not be the conventional thing to do, but it leaves the meat much more moist than plain roasting, and at the same time produces a good flavour. For a brace of pheasants, double the spice but keep the other boiling ingredients the same. The sauce may be doubled or increased by half.

    1 large pheasant

    Boiling
    1 tsp black peppercorns, crushed
    ½ tsp allspice berries, crushed
    ½ tsp juniper berries, crushed
    1 celery stick, roughly chopped
    1 carrot, roughly chopped

1 medium onion, roughly chopped
bouquet garni

Sauce
1 head celery
1 tbsp wholewheat flour
¼ pint (150 ml) dry white wine

Truss the pheasant. Put it into a saucepan with the boiling ingredients. Pour in cold water to just above the legs. Bring to the boil, skim and simmer for 1 hour or until the pheasant is tender. Take the pan from the heat but keep the pheasant in the liquid.

Finely chop the celery. In another saucepan, bring ¼ pint (150 ml) of the pheasant stock to the boil. Add the celery and cook, uncovered, over a medium heat until all the stock has reduced to a glaze.

Stir in the flour and then another ½ pint (275 ml) more of the stock. Bring to the boil, stirring. Simmer, uncovered, for 15 minutes. Add the wine and simmer for a further 2 minutes.

Joint the pheasant and arrange it on a serving dish. Remove the skin if preferred – it will come off very easily. Pour the celery sauce over the pheasant before serving.

Vegetarian and Vegetable Main Courses

Vegetarian cooking is no longer the Cinderella of cuisine. In recent years, once we realized that too much meat was not good for us, it has been 'rediscovered', broadened and made popular. Where once a couple of bags of red lentils and butter beans were stuck on the back of the supermarket shelf, now there are rows of many different varieties of pulses, nuts and grains. Wholefood shops are springing up everywhere offering even more choice. There are vegetarian books, vegetarian courses and vegetarian cookery schools, all teaching us how to enjoy cooking and eating without meat.

Pulses (dried beans, peas and lentils) have come to symbolize vegetarian cooking. They are a high protein food, containing some of the B vitamins (although not B_{12}), iron, potassium and calcium, plus a high percentage of fibre. The protein contained in pulses is not what has come to be termed a first-class protein. Proteins are made up of substances called amino acids which are linked together in chains. Those protein chains present in meat, fish, eggs and cheese have every amino acid that we need. Those contained in pulses have several links of the chain missing. However, the protein in wholegrains contains those amino acids which are missing from the beans. Therefore, pulses should always be eaten with a wholegrain if the dish in which they are included contains no animal protein. The simplest example is beans on wholewheat toast. Beans can also be served or cooked with wholewheat pasta, brown rice, millet, barley, oats, buckwheat or cornmeal.

The only drawback to cooking with pulses is the time they take to soak and cook. Lentils, either split or whole, need no soaking and will usually soften in 50 minutes or less; the same applies to split peas; but beans must be soaked. The best way to do this is to cover them with water, bring them to the boil and boil them for 10 minutes. Remove them from the heat and leave them for about 2 hours. After that, drain, add fresh cold water and 1 tbsp oil (this gives them a nice glossy appearance), bring to the boil, cover and simmer until tender.

Mung beans need 45 minutes; black eyed beans and adzuki beans, 1 hour; pinto beans, 1¼ hours; black, red and brown kidney beans, cannellini beans, flageolets and haricot beans, 1½ hours; chick peas, butter beans and dried broad beans, 2 hours; and soya beans, 3 to 4 hours. If you have a pressure cooker the time can be cut down considerably.

Beans can be made into casseroles with vegetables or meat, simmered gently with stock or another liquid and herbs or spices, and used in salads.

Nuts are another 'typically' vegetarian ingredient. They are small pieces of concentrated goodness and are another high protein food which must be served with grains. All are high in phosphorus (which works with B vitamins), potassium and iron, and they are an excellent source of calcium. Almonds, brazil nuts, pine kernels, peanuts and pistachio nuts are high in B vitamins and sunflower seeds in vitamins A and D. Some vitamin C is found in cashew nuts and vitamin E in chestnuts.

Besides being made into the familiar nut roasts, nuts can be stir-fried with vegetables, scattered over bean and/or vegetable casseroles, put into stuffings, made into pies and used in salads.

Some egg and cheese dishes are also included in this chapter. Although eggs have come in for some criticism lately because of their cholesterol content, they also contain lecithin, a substance which helps to disperse the cholesterol in the body. They are a high protein food, needing no accompaniment, and contain iron, B vitamins (including B12), vitamins A and D, calcium, potassium and magnesium. Of course, if you fry or scramble eggs frequently you are bound to add unnecessarily to your fat intake, but if you bake them, poach them or boil them an average of four a week should do you no harm.

Cheese provides protein, calcium, vitamins A and D and some B vitamins. Unfortunately, most hard cheeses have a high fat content so only use them fairly sparingly. It is best to buy farmhouse or other mature types of cheese rather than the milder ones, as you will need to use less of them. The Tendale cheeses which have recently come on to the market are made to taste and cook like traditional Cheddar and Cheshire cheeses without the high fat content. They taste mild when you first buy them but after being kept in the refrigerator for a week they become stronger. If you enjoy cheese meals these are well worth considering.

Bean and Red Leicester Bake

This rich, savoury, satisfying dish is best served with jacket potatoes.

> 8 oz (225 g) flageolets or haricot beans, soaked
> 1¼ pints (725 ml) stock
> bouquet garni
> 1 oz (25 g) butter or vegetable margarine
> 1 tbsp flour
> 2 tsp paprika
> 1 tbsp tomato purée
> ¼ tsp Tabasco sauce
> 1 tbsp chopped thyme
> 1 tbsp chopped parsley
> 8 oz (225 g) tomatoes
> 6 oz (175 g) red Leicester cheese
> 2 tbsp wheatgerm

Drain the soaked beans, discarding the liquid. Put the beans into a saucepan with the stock and bouquet garni. Bring to the boil, cover and simmer them until they are tender (1½ to 2 hours). Drain the beans again, reserving the stock.

Preheat the oven to 400°F (200°C/gas 6). Melt the butter or margarine in a saucepan over a moderate heat. Stir in the flour and paprika and cook for 1 minute. Stir in the tomato purée and then the stock. Bring the stock to the boil, stirring, and simmer it for 2 minutes. Add the Tabasco sauce and the herbs. Fold the beans into the sauce. Scald, skin and slice the tomatoes and finely grate the cheese.

Put half the beans into a large pie dish and cover them with half the cheese. Cover this with the slices of tomato and then put in another third of the cheese. Put in the rest of the beans and cover them with the remaining cheese. Scatter the wheatgerm over the top.

Put the dish into the oven for 25 minutes until the beans are covered with a layer of creamy melting cheese and crisp, browned wheatgerm.

Black Eyed Beans with Mixed Vegetables

This dish has a light flavour but it makes a very satisfying meal when served with rice or another whole grain.

> 8 oz (225 g) black eyed beans
> 1 lb (450 g) tomatoes
> 8 oz (225 g) courgettes
> 1 red pepper
> 1 green pepper
> 2 tbsp oil
> 1 large onion, thinly sliced
> 1 clove garlic, finely chopped
> ½ tsp ground coriander
> 2 tbsp white wine vinegar

Soak the beans. Boil them for 15 minutes and drain. Preheat the oven to 350°F (180°C/gas 4). Chop the tomatoes (scald and skin them first if preferred). Thinly slice the courgettes. Core and seed the peppers and cut them into 1 inch (2.5 cm) strips.

Heat the oil in a large flameproof casserole dish over a low heat. Add the onion and garlic and soften. Stir in the tomatoes, courgettes, peppers and coriander. Add the vinegar and bring to the boil. Stir in the beans. Cover the casserole and cook in the oven for 1 hour or until the beans are soft.

Serve either plain or topped with grated Cheddar cheese.

Brown Bean Winter Casserole

This makes a rich, warm-coloured casserole.

> 12 oz (350 g) carrots
> 12 oz (350 g) swede
> 12 oz (350 g) parsnips
> 2 medium onions
> 2 tbsp oil

8 oz (225 g) brown kidney beans or pinto beans,
    soaked and drained
1 pint (575 ml) stock
2 tbsp tomato purée
4 sage leaves, chopped
2 tbsp chopped thyme

Preheat the oven to 350°F (180°C/gas 4). Dice the carrots, swede and parsnips and finely chop the onions.

Heat the oil in a flameproof casserole dish over a low heat. Add the onions and soften them. Stir in the carrots, swede, parsnips and beans. Pour in the stock and bring it to the boil. Add the tomato purée and herbs.

Cover the casserole and cook in the oven for 1½ hours or until the beans are soft and most of the stock has been absorbed.

Butter Bean Goulash

Butter beans have a delicious creamy texture which goes well with the gentle flavours of paprika and soured cream.

12 oz (350 g) carrots
4 large celery sticks
4 oz (125 g) mushrooms
2 tbsp oil
1 large onion, thinly sliced
1 clove garlic, finely chopped
2 tbsp paprika
8 oz (225 g) butter beans, soaked
1½ pints (850 ml) stock
4 tbsp chopped parsley
1 bayleaf
¼ pint (150 ml) soured cream

Preheat the oven to 350°F (180°C/gas 4). Thinly slice the carrots. Chop the celery. Thinly slice the mushrooms.

Heat the oil in a flameproof casserole dish over a low heat. Add the onion and garlic and soften. Stir in the paprika and cook, stirring, for 1 minute being careful not to let it brown. Stir in the rest of the vegetables and the beans. Pour in the stock and bring to the boil. Add the parsley and bayleaf. Cover the casserole and cook it in the oven for 2 hours or until the beans are completely soft.

Stir in the soured cream. Cover the casserole again and leave it to stand for 10 minutes before serving.

Soya Beans, Cabbage and Caraway

> 12 oz (350 g) tomatoes
> 1 Savoy cabbage or other green cabbage
> 2 tbsp oil
> 1 large onion, thinly sliced
> 1 clove garlic, finely chopped
> 8 oz (225 g) soya beans, soaked and cooked
> ½ tsp caraway seeds
> ¼ pint (150 ml) natural yoghurt

Scald, skin and chop the tomatoes. Shred the cabbage. Heat the oil in a large saucepan over a low heat. Add the onion and garlic and soften. Stir in the cabbage, tomatoes, beans and caraway seeds. Cover and cook on a low heat for 20 minutes, or until the cabbage is just tender.

Stir in the yoghurt just before serving.

Green Lentils with Bean Sprouts

The fresh flavours of very quickly cooked bean sprouts and green pepper make a good contrast to musty flavoured lentils.

> 2 tbsp oil
> 1 large onion, thinly sliced
> 1 clove garlic, finely chopped
> 1 tsp ground ginger
> 8 oz (225 g) green lentils
> 1¼ pints (725 ml) stock
> 2 tbsp tamari or soy sauce
> 1 tbsp white wine vinegar
> 1 bayleaf

> 6 oz (175 g) bean sprouts
> 1 green pepper

Heat the oil in a saucepan over a low heat. Add the onion and garlic and soften. Stir in the ginger and lentils and cook, stirring, for 1 minute. Pour in the stock and bring it to the boil. Add the tamari or soy sauce, vinegar and bayleaf. Cover and cook gently for 1 hour or until the lentils are soft and nearly all the stock has been absorbed.

Core and seed the green pepper and cut into 1 inch (2.5 cm) strips. Add to the saucepan with the bean sprouts. Cover and cook for a further 5 minutes.

Chick Peas with Burghul and Peppers

A mixture of beans, wheat and vegetables makes this an all-in-one meal.

> 2 red peppers
> 2 green peppers
> 3 tbsp oil
> 1 large onion, finely chopped
> 1 clove garlic, finely chopped
> 1 tsp paprika
> 8 oz (225 g) burghul wheat (see page 125)
> 1 pint (575 ml) stock
> 8 oz (225 g) chick peas, soaked and cooked
> 4 tbsp chopped parsley
> juice ½ lemon, or more to taste
> natural yoghurt to serve (optional)

Core, seed and chop the peppers. Heat the oil in a saucepan over a low heat. Stir in the onion and garlic and soften. Stir in the paprika and burghul wheat and cook for 1 minute, still stirring. Pour in the stock and bring it to the boil. Add the chick peas, parsley and lemon juice. Cover and simmer for 20 minutes or until all the stock has been absorbed and the wheat is light and fluffy.

Taste and add extra lemon juice if required. Serve the yoghurt separately to spoon over the top.

Black Beans and Rice with Tomato Sauce

This is another all-in-one dish. All it needs as an accompaniment is a salad.

> 8 oz (225 g) black kidney beans
> 4 tbsp oil
> 2 medium onions, finely chopped
> 2 cloves garlic, finely chopped
> 1½ tsp ground cumin
> 1½ tsp ground coriander
> 1¼ pints (725 ml) stock
> pinch sea salt
> 12 oz (350 g) tomatoes
> 4 tbsp natural yoghurt

Soak the beans and cook them for 1 hour. Drain. Heat half the oil in a saucepan over a low heat. Stir in one onion, one clove of garlic and 1 tsp each of cumin and coriander. Cook until the onion is soft. Stir in the rice and cook it for 1 minute. Add the beans. Pour in the stock and bring to the boil. Add the salt. Cover and simmer for 45 minutes or until the rice and beans are tender and all the stock has been absorbed.

For the sauce, scald, skin and chop the tomatoes. Heat the remaining oil in a saucepan over a low heat. Stir in the remaining onion, garlic and spices and cook until the onion is soft. Add the tomatoes. Cook until they are reduced to a purée. Take the pan from the heat and when the sauce has come off the boil, stir in the yoghurt.

Put the beans and rice in a serving dish. Serve the sauce separately.

Chilli Bean Soup

This is a hot and warming soup for a main course.

> 8 oz (225 g) red kidney beans
> 2 red peppers

2 green peppers
2 tbsp oil
2 large onions, finely chopped
1 clove garlic, finely chopped
4 oz (125 g) long grain brown rice
¾ pint (425 ml) tomato juice
1½ pints (850 ml) stock
1 bayleaf
2 tsp Tabasco sauce

Soak the beans, boil them for 1 hour and drain. Core, seed and finely chop the peppers.

Heat the oil in a large saucepan over a low heat. Add the onions and garlic and soften. Add the peppers and rice and cook, stirring, for 2 minutes. Pour in the tomato juice and stock and bring to the boil. Add the bayleaf and Tabasco sauce. Cover and simmer for 45 minutes or until both rice and beans are tender.

Burghul and Red Bean Salad

Fresh herbs make this simple salad taste very special.

8 oz (225 g) burghul wheat (see page 125)
8 oz (225 g) red kidney beans, soaked and cooked
2 tbsp chopped mint
4 tbsp chopped parsley
1 tbsp chopped marjoram
1 tbsp chopped thyme
2 sage leaves, chopped
4 tbsp olive oil
2 tbsp white wine vinegar
1 clove garlic, crushed with a pinch sea salt
freshly ground black pepper

Soak the burghul wheat in warm water for 30 minutes. Drain and squeeze it dry. Put it into a bowl and mix in the beans and herbs.

Beat together the oil, vinegar, garlic and pepper and mix them into the salad.

Apricot and Chick Pea Salad

This is best served with a burghul salad. Any left over makes a
good first course.

> 8 oz (225 g) chick peas, soaked and simmered until
>   tender
> 8 fresh apricots, or dried whole apricots soaked
>   in orange juice for 6 hours and drained
> 2 tbsp sesame seeds
> 4 tbsp sesame oil or sunflower oil
> 1 large onion, quartered and thinly sliced
> 1 clove garlic, finely chopped
> juice ½ lemon
> ¼ pint (150 ml) natural yoghurt
> 2 tbsp tahini
> 4 tbsp chopped parsley

Put the sesame seeds into a heavy frying pan and toast them
over a moderate heat, stirring, until they brown. Tip them on to
a plate to cool.

Heat the oil in a saucepan over a low heat, add the onion and
garlic and cook until they are soft. Pour in the lemon juice and
let it bubble. Take the pan from the heat and allow to cool.

Beat the yoghurt with the tahini. Add the chick peas to the
onions and then fold in the yoghurt mixture. Stone and chop 6 of
the apricots and add them to the salad with the parsley. Turn
the salad into a serving dish. Stone and slice the remaining
apricots and use them as a garnish.

Pinto Bean and Egg Salad

> 4 hard-boiled eggs
> 1 green pepper
> 4 spring onions
> 8 oz (225 g) pinto beans, soaked and cooked
> 1 box mustard and cress

4 tbsp olive oil
juice ½ lemon
freshly ground black pepper

Finely chop the eggs. Core, seed and finely chop the pepper. Finely chop the spring onions. Mix all these with the beans and cut in the cress.

Beat the oil, lemon juice and pepper together and fold the resulting dressing into the salad.

Flageolet Salad with Avocado Dressing

1 ripe avocado
juice ½ lemon
4 tbsp olive oil
1 clove garlic, crushed with a pinch sea salt
8 oz (225 g) flageolets, soaked and cooked

Halve, stone, peel and mash the avocado. Gradually beat in the lemon juice and oil. Add the garlic and mix well. Mix in the beans.

The salad is best served immediately.

Yellow Pea and Apple Salad

Yellow peas don't have to be made into heavy pease puddings. This salad is light and tasty. Serve it with a green salad and wholewheat pitta or bread. The moulding and garnishing isn't essential, but a carefully presented meal is more appetizing than a splodge on the plate.

8 oz (225 g) yellow split peas
1 bayleaf
freshly ground black pepper
2 tbsp cider vinegar
4 tbsp olive oil or sunflower oil
1 small onion, very finely chopped
4 sage leaves, chopped

2 medium crisp dessert apples
little oil for greasing

Put the split peas into a saucepan with 1 pint (575 ml) water and the bayleaf. Bring to the boil, cover and simmer gently for 45 minutes, beating them for the last 10 minutes (after discarding the bayleaf) to make a thick purée. Take the pan from the heat and turn the purée into a bowl to cool.

Season the peas with plenty of pepper and then beat in the vinegar and oil. Thoroughly mix in the onion, sage leaves and one of the apples which you have cored and finely chopped.

Lightly grease either a ring mould or a bowl and press in the salad mixture.

Smooth the top and invert it on to a flat plate. Just before serving, core the remaining apple and cut it into thin lengthways slices. Use them to garnish the top of the mould.

Stir-fried Peppers and Walnuts

This rich, colourful walnut dish is best served with rice or wholewheat pasta.

2 medium red peppers
2 medium green peppers
4 tbsp olive oil
1 clove garlic, finely chopped
5 oz (150 g) chopped walnuts
1 tbsp chopped thyme
2 tbsp white wine vinegar

Core and seed the peppers and cut them into pieces about 1 × ¼ inch (2.5 cm × 6 mm).

Put the oil and garlic into a frying pan and set them on a high heat until the garlic begins to sizzle. Add the peppers and stir-fry them for 1 minute. Add the walnuts and stir-fry for 1 minute more. Mix in the thyme. Pour in the vinegar and let it bubble.

Take the pan from the heat and serve immediately.

Stir-fried Peanuts with Red Cabbage and Oranges

This dish has a light flavour and is best eaten with a rich grain such as a steamed brown rice or sautéed millet.

> ½ small to medium red cabbage
> 3 large oranges
> 2 tbsp white wine vinegar
> 1 clove garlic, crushed with a pinch sea salt
> pinch cayenne pepper
> 4 tbsp oil
> 1 large onion, thinly sliced
> 4 oz (125 g) shelled peanuts

Finely shred the cabbage. Squeeze the juice from one of the oranges and mix it with the vinegar, garlic and cayenne pepper. Cut the rind and pith from the remaining oranges, quarter them lengthways and thinly slice them.

Heat the oil in a large frying pan or wok over a medium heat. Add the onion and peanuts and stir until the onion is soft. Raise the heat. Add the cabbage and stir-fry it for 2 minutes or until it is just beginning to wilt. Add the oranges. Pour in the orange juice mixture and bring to the boil. Take the pan from the heat and serve immediately.

Buckwheat Spaghetti with Celery, Apple and Walnuts

> 4 oz (125 g) shelled walnuts
> 1 head celery
> 2 large onions
> 1 large cooking apple
> 2 tbsp oil
> 1 clove garlic, finely chopped
> 2 sage leaves, finely chopped
> 8 oz (225 g) buckwheat spaghetti
> 3 oz (75 g) Cheddar cheese, grated to serve (optional)

Finely grind the walnuts. Finely chop the celery and onion. Core and finely chop the apple.

Heat the oil in a large saucepan over a low heat. Add the celery, onion, apple, garlic and sage. Cook gently until the onion is soft and beginning to colour. Add the walnuts.

Cook the buckwheat spaghetti in lightly boiling salted water for 10 minutes. Drain. Gently fold it into the celery mixture.

Serve either plain or topped with grated cheese.

Savoury Pecan Pie

Crust
9 oz (250 g) rolled oats
2 tbsp wheatgerm
1 tbsp chopped thyme
1 tbsp chopped savory
2 sage leaves, chopped
1 tsp paprika
sea salt and freshly ground black pepper
3½ fl oz (100 ml) sunflower oil

Filling
2 tbsp sunflower oil
1 medium onion, thinly sliced
1 clove garlic, finely chopped
1 tsp paprika
1 small green cabbage
1 tbsp wholewheat flour
¼ pint (150 ml) stock
pinch sea salt
2 tbsp chopped thyme
1 tbsp chopped savory
2 sage leaves, chopped
4 oz (125 g) pecan nut halves
4 oz (125 g) Cheddar cheese

Preheat the oven to 400°F (200°C/gas 6). Put the rolled oats into a bowl and add the wheatgerm, herbs, paprika and seasonings. Mix in the oil. Press the rolled oat mixture on to the sides and base of a 10 inch (25 cm) diameter flan dish and bake for 20 minutes.

Meanwhile, heat the oil for the filling in a saucepan over a low heat. Add the onion, garlic and paprika and cook until the onion is soft. Mix in the cabbage, cover the pan and cook over a low heat for 5 minutes. Stir in the flour and cook it for ½ minute. Pour in the stock and bring to the boil. Simmer until it is thick, season and add the herbs. Take the pan from the heat.

Chop half the nuts and grate all the cheese. Mix the chopped nuts and half the cheese with the cabbage and put the mixture in the baked rolled oat case. Scatter the remaining cheese over the cabbage and arrange the remaining nuts in a pattern on top.

Return the pie to the oven for 15 minutes until the cheese melts and the pecan halves begin to brown. Serve hot.

Nutty Lentil and Tomato Loaf

This dish is moist, substantial and very tasty. It really needs no accompaniment except a salad. However, if you're really hungry, have jacket potatoes as well.

2 tbsp oil
2 large onions, finely chopped
1 clove garlic, finely chopped
6 oz (175 g) split red lentils
6 oz (175 g) millet
2 tsp curry powder
1 pint (575 ml) stock
1 tbsp tomato purée
2 tbsp chopped parsley
1 tbsp chopped thyme
2 oz (50 g) shelled walnuts
1 oz (25 g) shelled hazelnuts
1 oz (25 g) shelled brazil nuts
12 oz (350 g) tomatoes

Sauce
12 oz (350 g) tomatoes
2 tbsp oil
1 medium onion, finely chopped
1 clove garlic, finely chopped
2 celery sticks, finely chopped

1 tsp paprika
2 tsp malt vinegar
1 tsp molasses

Heat the oil in a saucepan over a low heat. Add the onions and garlic and soften. Stir in the lentils, millet and curry powder. Cook, stirring, for 1 minute. Pour in the stock and bring to the boil. Add the tomato purée, parsley and thyme. Cover and simmer for 40 minutes or until both lentils and millet are soft and all the stock absorbed.

Preheat the oven to 350°F (180°C/gas 4). Oil a 2 lb (900 g) loaf tin. Finely grind the nuts. Scald, skin and chop the tomatoes. Mix them both into the lentils and millet. Put the mixture into the loaf tin mounding it up slightly in the centre. Bake the loaf for 30 minutes. Turn it out of the tin.

To make the sauce, scald, skin and chop the tomatoes. Heat the oil in a saucepan over a low heat. Add the onion, garlic and celery and soften them. Stir in the tomatoes, paprika, vinegar and molasses. Cover and simmer for 10 minutes.

Serve the loaf hot, cut into slices and hand the sauce separately.

Nut Roast in a Dish

This is a very rich nut roast. Serve it with plenty of lightly cooked seasonal vegetables or with a salad. Potatoes or an extra grain dish shouldn't be necessary.

3 oz (75 g) shelled hazelnuts
3 oz (75 g) pine kernels or cashew nut pieces
3 oz (75 g) wholewheat bread
5 tbsp oil
3 large onions, thinly sliced
2 tsp yeast extract
¼ pint (150 ml) tomato juice
2 tbsp chopped parsley
1 tbsp chopped thyme
2 sage leaves, chopped

Preheat the oven to 350°F (180°C/gas 4). If you have a large liquidizer put in all the nuts and diced bread and grind them together. This will give a more interesting texture to the final result. If you have only a small liquidizer or grinder, do the nuts and crumbs separately.

Heat the oil in a frying pan over a low heat. Add the onions and soften. Mix in the yeast extract. Pour in the tomato juice and bring to the boil. Remove the pan from the heat and mix in the nuts, breadcrumbs and herbs.

Put the mixture into a small pie dish or soufflé dish. Bake in the oven for 45 minutes or until the top is crusty and brown.

Christmas Nut Roast

This stuffed nut roast would be suitable for a vegetarian Christmas dinner. Cranberry sauce, brussels sprouts and braised red cabbage are superb accompaniments. But, of course, you don't have to wait until Christmas to make it!

8 oz (225 g) grey or dark brown lentils
1 bayleaf
1 large onion, thinly sliced
4 oz (125 g) shelled walnuts
4 oz (125 g) shelled hazelnuts
4 oz (125 g) shelled brazil nuts
4 tbsp dry red wine
2 tbsp chopped thyme
2 tbsp chopped parsley
1 tbsp chopped savory
1 tsp chopped rosemary
sea salt and freshly ground black pepper

Stuffing
4 tbsp oil
1 large onion, quartered and thinly sliced
4 oz (125 g) wholewheat breadcrumbs
8 sage leaves, chopped
sea salt and freshly ground black pepper
6 tbsp dry red wine

Finishing
3 oz (75 g) wholewheat breadcrumbs
2 tbsp sesame seeds
4 tbsp oil

Boil the lentils with the bayleaf and onion until they are very tender. Drain, remove the bayleaf and mash the lentils and onion to a purée.

Preheat the oven to 400°F (200°C/gas 6). Chop the nuts very finely or grind them in a blender or mill. Mix the nuts into the lentil purée, together with the wine, herbs and seasonings.

To make the stuffing, heat the oil in a frying pan over a low heat. Add the onion and cook until it is soft. Take the pan from the heat and mix in the breadcrumbs, sage, seasonings and red wine.

In a long, flat, ovenproof dish, lay a base of half the lentil and nut mixture. Put all the stuffing on top. Cover the stuffing with the remaining nut mixture and form the whole into a long, humped shape with the stuffing completely enclosed. For coating the roast, mix together the breadcrumbs, sesame seeds and sunflower oil and press the mixture evenly over the surface.

Bake in the oven for 45 minutes until the crumbs on the outside are crisp and brown.

Celery, Hazelnut and Cheese Salad

With a rice or burghul salad this makes a substantial main meal.

    1 head celery
    4 oz (125 g) shelled hazelnuts
    2 oz (50 g) sultanas
    8 oz (25 g) curd cheese
    4 to 6 tbsp natural yoghurt
    1 clove garlic, crushed with a pinch sea salt
    freshly ground black pepper

Finely dice the celery and mix it in a salad bowl with the hazelnuts and sultanas. In a small bowl, beat the cheese to a cream and beat in 4 tbsp of the yoghurt. If the mixture is still very thick beat in another 2 tbsp. Add the garlic and pepper. Mix the cheesy dressing into the salad.

Curried Alfalfa and Almond Salad

Alfalfa is very rich and is best with spicy and sharp flavours. In this recipe the almonds turn yellow and become slightly curry flavoured. It's a dish which is both refreshing and filling at the same time.

> 6 oz (175 g) sprouted alfalfa
> 8 oz (225 g) almonds, blanched
> 3 oz (75 g) dried whole apricots
> 2 tsp curry powder
> 2 tsp ground cumin
> 6 tbsp olive oil
> grated rind and juice 1 lemon
> 1 clove garlic, crushed with a pinch sea salt

Divide the alfalfa between 4 serving plates. Quarter the apricots.

Put the curry powder and cumin into a bowl and gradually work in the oil. Beat in the lemon rind and juice and the garlic. Mix in the almonds and apricots and let them stand for 20 minutes to absorb the flavour of the dressing.

Arrange them on top of the alfalfa.

Endive and Mixed Nut Salad

> 1 medium curly endive
> 3 tbsp sesame seeds
> 4 tbsp olive oil
> 2 tbsp cider vinegar
> 1 clove garlic, crushed with a pinch sea salt
> freshly ground black pepper
> freshly grated nutmeg
> 2 oz (50 g) chopped walnuts
> 2 oz (50 g) shelled almonds
> 2 oz (50 g) shelled hazelnuts

2 oz (50 g) sunflower seeds
2 oz (50 g) chopped dates

Break the endive into small pieces. Put it into a bowl with the
sesame seeds. Make the dressing by beating together the oil,
vinegar, garlic, pepper and nutmeg. Fold it into the endive and
sesame seeds.

Divide the dressed salad between 4 bowls and scatter the nuts
and dates over the top.

Marrow Stuffed with Walnuts and Hazel Nuts

1 large marrow
2 oz (50 g) shelled walnuts
2 oz (50 g) shelled hazelnuts
6 oz (175 g) open mushrooms
1 medium cooking apple
3 tbsp oil
1 large onion, finely chopped
1 clove garlic, finely chopped
4 oz (125 g) buckwheat
4 oz (125 g) millet
1 pint (575 ml) stock
1 bayleaf
sea salt and freshly ground black pepper
4 tbsp chopped parsley
1 tbsp chopped thyme
4 sage leaves, chopped

Sauce
6 oz (175 g) open mushrooms
8 oz (225 g) tomatoes
4 tbsp oil
1 small onion, finely chopped
1 clove garlic, finely chopped
3 tbsp wholewheat flour
¾ pint (425 ml) stock
bouquet garni
sea salt and freshly ground black pepper

Preheat the oven to 400°F (200°C/gas 6). Slice both ends off the marrow and remove all the seeds and pith from the centre. Finely chop or grind the nuts. Finely chop the mushrooms. Peel, core and finely chop the apple. Heat the oil in a saucepan or large frying pan over a low heat. Add the onion and garlic and soften. Stir in the mushrooms and cook for 1 minute. Stir in the buckwheat and millet. Pour in the stock and bring it to the boil. Season and add the bayleaf. Cover the pan and simmer the grains for 20 minutes until they are soft and fluffy and all the stock has been absorbed.

Remove the pan from the heat. Discard the bayleaf. Mix in the apple and chopped herbs. Fill the marrow with the stuffing. Put it on a rack in a roasting tin and bake it for 1 hour.

Meanwhile, make the sauce. Finely chop the mushrooms and tomatoes. Heat the oil in a saucepan over a low heat. Add the onion, garlic and mushrooms and cook until the onion is soft. Stir in the flour. Stir in the stock and bring it to the boil. Add the tomatoes and bouquet garni and season. Simmer gently, un-covered, for 30 minutes, skimming if necessary. Strain the sauce and return it to the cleaned pan. Simmer for a further 5 minutes.

To serve the marrow, cut it into thick slices. Serve the hot sauce separately.

Peas and Beans with Ham

> 3 lbs (1.25 kg) broad beans (weighed before shelling)
> 3 lbs (1.25 kg) peas (weighed before shelling)
> 1 oz (25 g) butter
> 1 large onion, quartered and thinly sliced
> ½ pint (275 ml) ham stock
> 2 tbsp chopped summer savory
> 2 tbsp chopped chervil
> 12 oz (350 g) cooked lean ham

Shell the beans and peas. Melt the butter in a saucepan over a low heat. Add the onion and soften. Fold in the beans and peas. Pour in the stock and bring to the boil. Add the herbs. Cover and cook over a moderate heat for 10 minutes.

Cut the ham into ¾ inch (2 cm) dice. Mix it into the beans

and peas, cover, lower the heat and cook for a further 5 minutes.
Serve with new potatoes, plainly boiled in their skins.

Gilded Cauliflower

Gilded cauliflower looks really attractive. For extra flavour, non
vegetarians can add 4 oz (125 g) cooked lean ham, finely diced, to
the eggs and herbs.

> 1 large cauliflower
> 1 sprig thyme
> 4 sage leaves
> 6 eggs
> 2 tbsp chopped parsley
> 2 tbsp chopped thyme
> little butter for greasing

Preheat the oven to 400°F (200°C/gas 6). Trim the cauliflower
and steam it whole with the sprig of thyme and 2 of the sage
leaves for 15 minutes, or until a skewer will easily pierce it.

Beat the eggs. Chop the remaining 2 sage leaves. Mix them
into the eggs together with the parsley and thyme.

Put the whole cauliflower into a lightly buttered ovenproof
dish which is only slightly larger than the cauliflower. Pour the
egg mixture over it, making sure that most of the herbs stay on
top of the cauliflower.

Bake the cauliflower in the oven for 20 minutes so the eggs set
to make a golden coat over it and ruff around it.

Stuffed Avocados

> 4 medium avocados, ripe but still quite firm
> 6 hard-boiled eggs
> 4 oz (125 g) lean bacon
> 3 oz (75 g) wholewheat breadcrumbs
> 4 oz (125 g) Cheddar cheese, grated
> 3 tbsp chopped chives
> freshly ground black pepper

Preheat the oven to 400°F (200°C/gas 6). Halve, stone and peel the avocados and lay the halves in an ovenproof serving dish. Peel and chop the eggs. Grill the bacon rashers under a high grill so they are cooked through but not crisp, then finely chop them.

In a bowl, pound the chopped hard-boiled eggs to a paste with the breadcrumbs. Then mix in the cheese, bacon and chives and season with the pepper. Press the stuffing on top of the avocados. It will be piled quite high but it sticks together well so it won't fall off.

Bake the avocados for 20 minutes until the top of the stuffing is a golden brown.

Courgette, Tomato and Green Pepper Soup

1 lb (450 g) courgettes
12 oz (350 g) tomatoes
2 medium green peppers
4 tbsp olive oil
1 large onion, finely chopped
1 clove garlic, finely chopped
2 tsp paprika
¼ tsp cayenne pepper
2 pints (1.15 l) stock
2 oz (50 g) very small pasta shapes
4 oz (125 g) Cheddar or Gruyère cheese

Finely chop the courgettes. Scald, skin and chop the tomatoes. Core, seed and chop the peppers.

Heat the oil in a large saucepan over a low heat. Add the onion, garlic, paprika and cayenne pepper. Cook for 1 minute. Stir in the courgettes, tomatoes and green peppers. Cover the pan and cook the vegetables gently for 10 minutes. Pour in the stock and bring it to the boil. Add the pasta shapes. Cover the pan and simmer the soup for 15 minutes.

To serve: pour the soup into deep bowls and float the cheese on the top.

Cheese and Aubergine Bake

A light salad is the best accompaniment to this rich all-in-one dish.

> 1½ lbs (675 g) aubergines
> 2 tbsp sea salt
> 2 medium green peppers
> 1 lb (450 g) firm tomatoes
> up to 8 tbsp olive oil
> 1 large onion, thinly sliced
> 1 clove garlic, finely chopped
> 8 oz (225 g) Mozzarella cheese
> 2 tbsp wholewheat flour
> 4 eggs, beaten
> ¼ pint (150 ml) natural yoghurt
> 2 oz (50 g) cheddar cheese, grated

Cut the aubergine into ½ inch (1.5 cm) slices. Put them into a colander and sprinkle with sea salt and leave to drain for 30 minutes. Rinse them in cold water and dry with kitchen paper.

Preheat the oven to 400°F (200°C/gas 6). Core and seed the peppers and cut them into pieces 1 × ¼ inch (2.5 cm × 6 mm). Scald and skin and slice the tomatoes.

Heat 2 tbsp of the oil in a frying pan over a moderate heat. Add enough aubergine slices to cover the pan and cook them till they are a translucent green on both sides. Cook the rest in the same way, adding more oil when necessary. Remove all the aubergines from the pan and lower the heat. Put in the onion, garlic and peppers and cook until they are soft. Remove the pan from the heat.

Thinly slice the Mozzarella cheese. Beat the flour, eggs, yoghurt and Cheddar cheese together. Put half the aubergines into the bottom of a large, greased ovenproof dish, then half the onions and peppers and half the tomatoes. Cover them with the Mozzarella and then repeat the layers in the opposite order, ending with aubergines. Pour the yoghurt mixture over the top.

Cook in the oven for 30 minutes so the topping is firm and golden brown. Serve straight from the dish.

Barley Bake with Smoked Cheddar

Ordinary Cheddar cheese can be used for this but the smoked type really does give it a special flavour.

> 1 small head celery
> 2 red peppers
> 2 tbsp oil
> 1 large onion, thinly sliced
> 1 clove garlic, finely chopped
> 8 oz (225 g) pot barley
> pinch cayenne pepper
> 1 pint (575 ml) stock
> 4 tbsp chopped parsley
> 2 oz (50 g) watercress
> 4 oz (125 g) smoked Cheddar cheese, finely grated

Preheat the oven to 350°F (180°C/gas 4). Finely chop the celery. Core, seed and finely chop the peppers. Heat the oil in a flameproof casserole dish over a low heat. Add the celery, onion and peppers and cook them, stirring occasionally, until the onion is soft. Stir in the barley and cayenne pepper. Pour in the stock and bring to the boil. Add the parsley. Cover the casserole and cook it in the oven for 1 hour or until the barley is tender and all the stock absorbed.

Finely chop the watercress. Fork it into the barley together with the cheese.

Potato and Cheese Bake

> 1½ lbs (675 g) small potatoes
> 1 oz (25 g) butter
> 1 large onion, thinly sliced
> 4 oz (125 g) Cheddar cheese, grated
> ¼ nutmeg, grated
> 4 tbsp chopped parsley
> sea salt and freshly ground black pepper
> 1 clove garlic, crushed with a pinch sea salt

¾ pint (425 ml) milk
5 tbsp soured cream
1 bayleaf

Preheat the oven to 350°F (180°C/gas 4). Scrub the potatoes and cut them into ⅛ inch (3 mm) slices. Melt half the butter in a frying pan over a low heat. Add the onion and soften it. Remove the pan from the heat.

Use the remaining butter to grease a deep ovenproof dish. Layer the potatoes, onions and two-thirds of the cheese in the casserole, adding nutmeg, parsley and seasonings as you go. Finish with a layer of potatoes and do not season the top. Beat the garlic into the milk. Add the soured cream and mix well. Pour the mixture into the casserole. Add the bayleaf.

Bake in the oven for 1 hour, pushing the potatoes back under the milk after the first 30 minutes. Scatter the remaining cheese over the top and cook in the oven for a further 20 minutes until the cheese melts and begins to brown.

Mixed Beetroot Salad with Cheese Dressing

12 oz (350 g) beetroot, cooked
1 lb (450 g) new potatoes, cooked
8 oz (225 g) shelled broad beans, cooked,
    or 4 oz (125 g) haricot beans, soaked and cooked
2 large pickled gherkins
4 oz (125 g) fromage blanc
6 tbsp mayonnaise
juice ½ lemon
freshly ground black pepper

Dice the beetroot and potatoes and mix them with the beans. Finely chop the gherkins and add them to the rest.

Beat together the remaining ingredients to make the dressing. Fold into the salad.

Mixed Avocado and Cheese Salad

This substantial salad is best served with a salad of burghul wheat or brown rice.

> 2 avocados
> 8 oz (225 g) Cheshire cheese
> 1 lb (450 g) tomatoes
> 4 small ridge cucumbers, or ½ large ordinary
>   cucumber
> 6 large salad onions
> 2 oz (50 g) sunflower seeds
> 1 oz (25 g) sesame seeds
> 4 tbsp olive oil
> 2 tbsp white wine vinegar
> 1 tbsp tomato purée
> 2 drops Tabasco sauce
> 1 clove garlic, crushed with a pinch sea salt
> 2 tbsp chopped basil if available
> 1 medium lettuce

Peel and stone the avocados and chop them into ½ inch (1.5 cm) dice. Chop the cheese, tomatoes and cucumbers into pieces the same size, and finely chop the onions. Put all these into a bowl with the sunflower and sesame seeds.

Beat the oil, vinegar, tomato purée, Tabasco sauce, garlic and basil together and mix the resulting dressing into the salad.

Line a serving bowl with lettuce leaves and pile the salad in the centre.

Eggs Baked with Mushrooms

This is a very easy dish to prepare. The mushrooms provide a succulent savoury base for the eggs.

> 8 eggs
> 1 oz (25 g) butter or vegetable margarine
> 8 oz (225 g) mushrooms

4 tbsp chopped parsley
4 fl oz (125 ml) soured cream

Heat the oven to 400°F (200°C/gas 6). Put a knob of butter into a flat ovenproof dish and place in the oven for 2 minutes so that the butter melts.

Finely chop the mushrooms and mix them into the butter. Break the eggs into the dish, sprinkle them with the parsley and pour over the soured cream.

Bake the eggs for 15 minutes so that the whites are set and the yolks still liquid.

Egg Bake with Pepper and Cheese Topping

In texture, this is a cross between a soufflé and an omelette. It is very colourful and looks impressive.

4 eggs, separated
1 tbsp chopped thyme
1 tbsp chopped parsley
freshly ground black pepper
little butter for greasing

Topping
2 medium green peppers
4 tbsp olive oil
2 medium onions, thinly sliced
1 clove garlic, finely chopped
8 oz (225 g) tomatoes
6 oz (175 g) Edam cheese
approx 2 tbsp tomato purée

Preheat the oven to 400°F (200°C/gas 6). First of all prepare the topping. Core and seed the peppers and cut them into strips about 1 × ¼ inch (2.5 cm × 6 mm). Heat the oil in a frying pan over a low heat. Add the peppers, onions and garlic and cook them until the onions are soft. Take them from the heat. Scald and skin the tomatoes and cut them into thin, crossways slices.

Beat the egg yolks with the herbs and pepper. Stiffly whip the egg whites and fold in the yolks with a metal spoon. Put the egg mixture into a buttered 10 inch (25 cm) diameter flat ovenproof dish and smooth the top. Bake for 15 minutes or until it is almost set but not brown.

Cut the cheese into thin, triangular slices. Remove the egg mixture from the oven and cover it first with the peppers and then the tomato slices. Put the cheese on top of the tomatoes and spread the tomato purée over it. Bake in the oven for a further 15 minutes.

Tuna Roulade

    3½ oz (100 g) tin tuna
    6 green olives
    4 large eggs, separated
    4 oz (125 g) open mushrooms
    2 tbsp olive oil
    1 tbsp grated Parmesan cheese

Preheat the oven to 400°F (200°C/gas 6). Drain and flake the tuna. Stone and chop the olives. Line a swiss roll tin with oiled greaseproof paper.

Mix the tuna and olives with the egg yolks. Stiffly whip the egg whites and fold them into the tuna, olive and yolk mixture. Spread over the greaseproof paper and bake for 12 minutes so that it sets and just begins to brown.

While this is cooking, lightly brush the mushrooms with oil. Grill them and chop them.

Scatter the mushrooms and Parmesan cheese over the roulade. Roll up the roulade from one narrow end, gently lifting the paper to help you. Tip the roulade on to a warm serving plate. Extra Parmesan cheese can be sprinkled over the top if wished.

Peanut-coated Eggs

    8 small eggs
    3 tbsp oil
    1 medium onion, finely chopped
    1 clove garlic, finely chopped

2 tsp hot Madras curry powder
8 oz (225 g) split red lentils
2 tbsp chopped parsley
1 tbsp chopped thyme
1 tsp chopped rosemary
3 oz (75 g) shelled peanuts
2 oz (50 g) wholewheat flour
1 egg, beaten
deep oil for frying

Hard-boil the eggs and cool them. Heat the oil in a saucepan over a low heat. Stir in the onion and garlic and soften. Stir in the curry powder and lentils and cook for 1 minute. Pour in 1 pint (575 ml) water and bring to the boil. Add the herbs. Cover and simmer for 45 minutes or until the water has been absorbed and the lentils can be beaten to a purée.

Finely grind the nuts in a grinder or liquidizer. Mix them into the lentils. Leave the mixture until it is cold and firm.

Coat each egg in the peanut mixture. Roll them first in wholewheat flour, then in the beaten egg and once again in the flour. Heat a deep pan of oil to 375°F (190°C). Add the eggs, two at a time, and cook for 2 minutes until golden brown all over. Lift them on to kitchen paper and drain. Serve them hot or cold.

Vegetable Accompaniments

It would be very difficult to maintain a healthy, balanced diet without vegetables. They contain a wide variety of vitamins and minerals and a high percentage of fibre. It would also be difficult to make enjoyable meals without them. Just think of all those interesting shapes, textures and flavours to be made use of raw or cooked, alone or in combinations. How boring your meals would look without them!

Most vegetables contain vitamin C, some to a greater extent than others. It is found in large amounts in all the green vegetables, such as broccoli, kale, brussels sprouts, green peppers, cabbage, cauliflower, spinach and watercress. It is also found in root vegetables and the humble potato. Vitamin A is found in red vegetables such as red peppers, carrots and pumpkin and, to a lesser extent, in dark green vegetables such as broccoli, kale and watercress. Some vegetables contain B vitamins and vitamin K is found in green vegetables. All vegetables contain minerals, particularly calcium and potassium.

Since vegetables vary in the types and amounts of nutrients that they contain, try to make sure that you eat a wide variety every day. It is a good idea to have one salad meal and one meal including cooked vegetables. The salad, for example, could contain watercress, tomatoes, celery and beetroot and the cooked meal could be accompanied by carrots, a green vegetable and potatoes.

Choose different vegetables every day, alternating the exotic with the more ordinary, and try to vary your cooking methods. That way, vegetables can always be an enjoyable as well as important part of any meal.

Runner Beans and Worcester Sauce

> 1 lb (450 g) runner beans
> 1 tbsp Worcestershire sauce
> 1 tbsp olive oil
> 4 tbsp stock
> 4 tbsp chopped parsley

String the beans and chop them into ½ inch (1.5 cm) lengths. Put the Worcestershire sauce, oil and stock into a saucepan. Bring to the boil and stir in the beans and parsley.

Cover the pan and leave it on a moderate heat for 15 minutes. The beans should be just tender and a dark, shiny green and most of the liquid should have evaporated.

Broad Beans and Tomatoes

If savory or basil are not available, try using parsley or thyme instead.

> 3 lb (1.25 kg) broad beans (weighed before shelling)
> 1 lb (450 g) ripe tomatoes
> 1 tbsp chopped savory
> 1 tbsp chopped basil

Shell the beans. Scald, skin and chop the tomatoes. Put the tomatoes and herbs into a saucepan. Cook, covered, over a low heat until the tomatoes begin to soften – about 4 minutes. Stir in the beans, cover again and cook for 20 minutes.

Braised Brussels Sprouts and Button Onions

Braising is probably the best way of cooking brussels sprouts. It makes them succulent but not over-soft and brings out their nutty flavour. It is also an excellent way of cooking baby onions.

They keep their shape but soften and mellow. Put the two together and you have a real luxury dish.

> ½ lb (225 g) brussels sprouts
> ½ lb (225 g) button onions
> ½ pint (275 ml) stock
> ½ tsp ground mace

Preheat the oven to 350°F (180°C/gas 4). Trim the sprouts and peel the onions. Bring half the stock to the boil in a flameproof casserole dish over a high heat. Add the onions and cook them until they look transparent and all the stock has evaporated.

Add the brussels sprouts. Pour in the remaining stock and bring to the boil. Sprinkle in the mace. Cover the casserole and cook it in the oven for 45 minutes.

Cabbage with Herbs and Garlic

Choose your herb to match your main dish.

> 1 green cabbage
> 1 small onion
> ½ oz (15 g) butter or vegetable margarine
> 1 clove garlic, finely chopped
> 2 tbsp chopped parsley
> 1 tbsp chopped savory, or thyme or fennel,
>   or 3 sage leaves, chopped

Shred the cabbage. Thinly slice the onion. Melt the butter in a saucepan over a high heat. Stir in the cabbage, onion, garlic and herbs. Pour in 6 tbsp water. Lower the heat, cover and cook gently for 15 minutes. Serve with pork or with egg dishes.

Summer Cabbage with New Apples

The apples will cook down until they are soft and pulpy and so will moisten and flavour the light, fresh textured cabbage.

1 medium summer cabbage
2 medium George Cave apples, or other early
   variety of dessert apple
4 tbsp oil

Shred the cabbage. Quarter, core and thinly slice the apples.
Heat the oil in a large saucepan over a high heat. Add the
cabbage and cook it for ½ minute. Mix in the apples. Cover
tightly and simmer gently for 15 minutes.

Cauliflower with Walnut Sauce

1 large cauliflower
1 oz (25 g) shelled walnuts
¼ pint (150 ml) stock
1 small onion, finely chopped
1 clove garlic, finely chopped
sea salt and freshly ground black pepper
2 tbsp chopped chervil or parsley

Break the cauliflower into small sprigs and steam them for 15
minutes or until just tender.

Prepare the sauce while the cauliflower is cooking. Finely
chop the walnuts. Put 4 tbsp of the stock into a small saucepan
and bring to the boil. Add the onion and garlic and boil them
gently until all the stock is reduced and the vegetables are
sticky and slightly golden in colour. Pour in the remaining
stock and bring to the boil.

Season, adding plenty of pepper, and put in the walnuts and
chervil. Simmer the sauce for 2 minutes. Place the cooked
cauliflower in a warm serving dish and spoon the sauce over the
top.

Braised Celery

1 small head celery
1 medium onion
4 oz (125 g) carrots
7 fl oz (200 ml) stock

6 tbsp dry white wine or more stock
1 tbsp tomato purée
2 tsp chopped thyme
1 clove garlic, finely chopped

Heat the oven to 350°F (180°C/gas 4). Cut the outer sticks of celery into pieces about 4 inches (10 cm) long. Keep the innermost sticks together and trim only the rough parts away from the crunchy root. Cut the remaining heart in half crossways and then the bottom part in half lengthways. Keep the inner leaves. Finely dice the onion and carrots.

Bring 4 fl oz (125 ml) of the stock to the boil in a flameproof casserole dish over a high heat. Stir in the onion and carrots and boil until all the stock has evaporated. Pour in the remaining stock and wine and bring to the boil. Stir in the tomato purée and mix in the thyme and garlic. Put in the celery and make sure it has carrots and onion above and below it.

Cover and cook in the oven for 50 minutes.

Alternative: omit the tomato purée and use cider and sage instead of wine and thyme.

Green Peppers with Grated Courgettes

This is a fresh, green mixture of summer vegetables.

3 medium green peppers
3 tbsp olive oil
1 large onion, finely chopped
1 clove garlic, finely chopped
1 lb (450 g) courgettes
2 tbsp chopped thyme

Core, seed and finely chop the peppers. Heat the oil in a saucepan over a low heat. Add the peppers, onion and garlic. Cover and simmer gently for 15 minutes.

In the meantime, wipe and coarsely grate the courgettes. Add them to the pepper mixture with the thyme. Cover again and simmer for a further 2 minutes.

Serve immediately or the mixture may go watery.

Braised Artichokes with Lemon and Parsley

Braised Jerusalem artichokes keep their shape but have a soft melty texture when you bite into them. Lemon makes a perfect contrast to their earthy flavour.

    1 lb (450 g) Jerusalem artichokes
    ½ pint (275 ml) stock
    1 medium onion, finely chopped
    grated rind and juice ½ lemon
    3 tbsp chopped parsley

Preheat the oven to 350°F (180°C/gas 4). Peel the artichokes, keeping them in a bowl of cold water to which you have added a squeeze of lemon juice or a dash of white wine vinegar. Cut them into ¾ inch (2 cm) pieces and leave them in the water until you are ready to cook them.

Put half the stock into a flameproof casserole dish and bring it to the boil over a high heat. Add the onion and cook until all the stock has evaporated.

Pour in the remaining stock and bring to the boil. Add the artichokes, lemon rind and juice and parsley. Cover the casserole and cook in the oven for 45 minutes.

Leeks and Parsnips in a Packet

The vegetables are lightly cooked and their flavours sealed into a packet.

    1 lb (450 g) leeks
    1 lb (450 g) parsnips
    ¾ oz (20 g) butter
    freshly ground black pepper

Preheat the oven to 400°F (200°C/gas 6). Wash the leeks well and thinly slice them. Scrub the parsnips. Cut away the woody cores if they are large and cut the rest into matchstick-sized pieces. Add them to the leeks.

Use a little of the butter to grease a piece of foil before putting the leeks and parsnips on it. Dot them with the remaining butter and season with the pepper. Seal the edges of the foil and put the parcel on a baking sheet. Cook in the oven for 45 minutes.

Tip the vegetables on to a warm dish to serve.

Steamed Marrow with Mint and Yoghurt

This is good with curry.

> 1 small marrow
> 3 tbsp chopped mint
> ¼ pint (150 ml) natural yoghurt

Peel and core the marrow. Cut it into small pieces, about 1 × ¼ inch (2.5 cm × 6 mm). Put them into a steamer and scatter in 2 tbsp of the mint. Lower the steamer over boiling water and steam, covered, for 15 minutes, turning the marrow pieces occasionally if they are several layers deep.

Drain well. Turn the marrow into a serving dish and gently mix in the yoghurt. Scatter the remaining mint over the top.

Baked Onions

Use medium-sized onions, one per person. Make sure they are clean but don't trim them.

Preheat the oven to 400°F (200°C/gas 6). Stand the onions on the oven rack and bake them for 1½ hours.

Serve in their skins as it is a real treat to pull back the outer peel and find the soft, sweet, yellow-tinged layers inside.

Butter, vegetable margarine, grated Cheddar cheese, curd cheese or fromage blanc can all be spooned inside once the onions are opened.

Peas with Marigolds and Marjoram

> 2 lbs (900 g) fresh green peas (weighed before shelling)
> ¼ pint (150 ml) stock
> 2 tbsp chopped marjoram
> petals from 4 marigold heads

Shell the peas. Put the stock into a saucepan and bring to the boil. Add the peas, marjoram and marigold petals. Cover and simmer for 15 minutes by which time the peas should be tender and most of the stock absorbed.

Steamed Potatoes with Onions and Nutmeg

Steamed potatoes stay moist and tasty and rarely go floury like boiled ones. The flavour's so good that they are delicious served quite plainly without being tossed in butter.

> 1½–2 lbs (675–900 g) medium old potatoes
> 1 large onion, quartered and thinly sliced
> ⅛ nutmeg, freshly grated
> freshly ground black pepper
> 1 bayleaf

Scrub the potatoes but don't peel them. Cut them into ¼ inch (6 mm) thick slices. Place them in a large vegetable steamer with the onions and seasonings and tuck in the bayleaf. Cover and steam for 30 minutes, turning the potatoes frequently so that they cook evenly.

Discard the bayleaf and turn into a warm serving dish.

Jacket Potatoes

These are the easiest of all potatoes to prepare and are probably the most nutritious since all the goodness is sealed in.

Preheat the oven to 400°F (200°C/gas 6). Scrub as many large potatoes as you need and prick each one twice on both sides with a fork. Lay the potatoes on the oven rack and bake them for 1¼ hours.

For serving, they can be slit open and topped with butter, vegetable margarine or cheese.

They are also good served plain with casserole-type dishes containing a generous amount of sauce.

Olive and Tomato Topping for Jacket Potatoes

This seems richer and tastier than butter but in fact is much lower in fats and calories.

> 8 black olives
> 4 oz (125 g) quark or other low fat soft cheese
> 1 tbsp tomato purée
> 2 tbsp soured cream

Stone and finely chop the olives. Pound them to a paste with a pestle and mortar. Cream the cheese in a bowl. Add the olives, tomato purée and soured cream and mix well.

Pile on top of jacket baked potatoes.

Hot in Two Ways Potato Salad

> 1½ lbs (675 g) small new potatoes
> 3 tbsp mayonnaise
> 1 tbsp white wine vinegar
> 1 tsp Tabasco sauce

Wash the potatoes and boil them whole in their skins until they are just tender. Drain and skin them when they are still hot.

Mix all the ingredients for the dressing together and put them into a saucepan. Turn the potatoes carefully in the dressing, taking care not to break them.

Set the pan, covered, over a low heat for about 1 minute, shaking once or twice, to heat the potatoes through again.

Pumpkin Casserole

This is a light and savoury casserole dish with a deliciously creamy texture. It will go with most savoury dishes.

> 2¼ lb (1 kg) slice pumpkin
> 2 tbsp chopped mixed fresh herbs
> sea salt and freshly ground black pepper
> ¼ pint (150 ml) stock
> 1 medium onion, thinly sliced

Preheat the oven to 400°F (200°C/gas 6). Cut the rind and seeds from the pumpkin and cut the flesh into small, thin slices. Place them in a small, lightly greased casserole, scattering in the herbs, a little salt and plenty of pepper as you go.

Put the stock and onion in a saucepan and bring to the boil. Pour over the pumpkin. Cover the casserole and cook it in the oven for 30 minutes.

Stir-fried Spinach with Paprika and Onions

Stir-frying spinach turns it into a glossy vegetable that is full of flavour.

> 1½ lbs (675 g) spinach
> 4 tbsp olive or sunflower oil
> 1 medium onion, quartered and thinly sliced
> 1 clove garlic, finely chopped
> 2 tsp paprika

Break the stems from the spinach where they join the leaves. Wash the leaves, dry them well and finely chop them.

Heat the oil in a large paella pan over a low heat. Add the onion and garlic and soften. Raise the heat to high and mix in the spinach and paprika. Cook the spinach briskly, turning it over all the time until it is just tender and all the moisture in the pan has been driven away.

Steamed, Grated Swede with Nutmeg and Worcestershire Sauce

> 12 oz (350 g) swede (weighed after trimming away
>   any knobbly bits and blemishes)
> 1 medium onion, finely chopped
> freshly grated nutmeg
> 2 tbsp chopped parsley
> 1 tbsp Worcestershire sauce
> 1 oz (25 g) butter or vegetable margarine (optional)

Scrub the swede and finely grate it. Place in a vegetable steamer. Mix in the onion and add a little freshly grated nutmeg. Steam, covered, for 20 minutes, turning several times.

Mix in the parsley and Worcestershire sauce. Taste it and add a little more nutmeg if necessary.

Butter or vegetable margarine can be beaten into the swede before serving if required.

Honeyed Turnips with Parsley

> 6 small turnips
> ½ oz (15 g) butter
> 1 medium onion, thinly sliced
> 2 tsp honey
> ¼ pint (150 ml) stock
> 4 tbsp chopped parsley

Preheat the oven to 350°F (180°C/gas 4). Peel the turnips. Cut each one in half lengthways and the halves crossways into ¼ inch (6 mm) slices.

Melt the butter in a flameproof casserole dish over a low heat. Add the onion and cook until it just begins to turn golden. Stir in the turnips. Add the honey and stir again. Cook gently for 2 minutes. Add the stock and bring to the boil. Mix in the parsley.

Cover the casserole and cook in the oven for 1 hour.

Serve with pork or lamb.

Baked Tomato Crumble

> 1½ lb (675 g) tomatoes
> 4 tbsp wheatgerm
> 2 tbsp grated Parmesan cheese
> 2 tbsp chopped parsley
> 1 tbsp chopped thyme
> little butter or oil for greasing small pie dish

Heat the oven to 350°F (180°C/gas 4). Scald and skin the tomatoes and slice them into rounds. Mix together the wheatgerm, cheese, parsley and thyme.

Arrange half the tomatoes in the bottom of a lightly greased pie dish. Sprinkle half the wheatgerm mixture on top. Lay in all the remaining tomatoes and top them with the rest of the wheatgerm. Bake for 20 minutes.

Alternatives: the cheese can be omitted; the thyme can be replaced with basil.

Cabbage, Fennel and Fruit Salad

> ½ small white cabbage
> 1 bulb fennel
> 4 oz (125 g) green grapes
> 2 satsumas
> 4 tbsp olive oil, or sunflower oil
> 2 tbsp cider vinegar
> 1 tsp spiced granular mustard

1 clove garlic, crushed with a pinch sea salt
freshly ground black pepper

Shred the cabbage and chop the fennel. Halve and seed the grapes and pull the satsumas into segments. Put them all together in a salad bowl.

Beat the oil, vinegar, mustard, garlic and pepper together to make the dressing and fold it into the salad.

Carrot, Watercress and Apple Salad

2 large carrots
2 bunches watercress
1 large Bramley apple
4 tbsp sunflower oil
2 tbsp cider vinegar
½ tsp ground ginger
1 clove garlic, crushed with a pinch sesame salt
freshly ground black pepper

Grate the carrots, chop the watercress, and quarter, core and chop the apple. Put them into a bowl.

Beat the remaining ingredients together to make the dressing and fold into the salad.

Chicory and Pepper Salad

8 oz (225 g) chicory
1 red pepper
1 yellow pepper
1 tbsp tahini
3 tsp sesame oil
2 tbsp cider vinegar
1 tbsp tomato purée
¼ tsp Tabasco sauce
1 clove garlic, crushed with a pinch sea salt

Halve the chicory bulbs lengthways and thinly slice them. Core and seed the peppers and cut them into 1 inch (2.5 cm) strips. Place them all in a salad bowl.

Put the tahini into a small bowl and gradually beat in first the oil and then the vinegar, tomato purée and Tabasco sauce. Add the garlic and mix well. Fold the resulting dressing into the salad.

Courgette and Pepper Salad

> 12 oz (350 g) courgettes
> 1 large red pepper
> 1 large green pepper
> 1 large onion
> 4 tbsp olive oil
> 1 clove garlic, finely chopped
> 2 tbsp white wine vinegar
> 4 tomatoes
> 12 anchovy fillets

Wipe and thinly slice the courgettes. Core and deseed the peppers and cut them into pieces 1 × ¼ inches (2.5 cm × 6 mm). Quarter and thinly slice the onion. Heat the oil in a saucepan over a low heat. Stir in the courgettes, peppers, onion and garlic. Cover and cook gently for 20 minutes. The vegetables should be only just tender. Take the pan from the heat and fold in the vinegar. Leave the salad until it is completely cold.

Scald, skin and slice the tomatoes. Gently mix them into the salad. Turn the salad into a flat serving dish. Cut the anchovy fillets in half lengthways and make a lattice pattern with them on top of the salad.

Summer Raspberry Salad

> 1 lettuce
> ½ large cucumber
> 4 oz (125 g) raspberries
> 4 tbsp chopped parsley
> 2 tsp chopped tarragon

4 sage leaves, chopped
6 spring onions, chopped
4 tbsp olive oil
2 tbsp tarragon vinegar
pinch sea salt
freshly ground black pepper

Shred the lettuce. Finely chop the cucumber. Put them into a salad bowl and add the raspberries and herbs.

Beat together the oil, vinegar and seasonings and fold the resulting dressing into the salad.

Tomato, Cucumber and Currant Salad

12 oz (350 g) tomatoes
1 small cucumber
4 tbsp natural yoghurt
1 tsp ground cinnamon
1 tbsp tomato purée
1 clove garlic, very finely chopped
2 oz (50 g) currants

Chop the tomatoes. Cut the cucumber into quarters lengthways and slice thinly. Place the tomatoes and cucumber in a salad bowl.

Beat the yoghurt, cinnamon, tomato purée and garlic together and fold them into the salad. Scatter the currants over the top.

Grains and Pastas

Wholegrains, for so long used in wholefood and vegetarian cooking, have suddenly become popular. The interest in high fibre diets is mainly responsible for this, but along with the fibre you are also getting more B vitamins, protein, minerals and vitamin E than you would on a diet of refined grain products such as white rice and white pasta. Wholegrain foods should not be treated as a passing fad. They should become a favourite and permanent part of the store-cupboard.

As with most healthy foods, the natural kinds actually taste better, or to put it more truthfully perhaps, they actually *taste*, whereas the white kinds provide bulk but little flavour.

Brown rice is widely available. It takes longer to cook than white rice (40 to 45 minutes as opposed to 15 to 20 minutes) but it is easy to get perfect results every time since the outer coating of bran prevents the grains from sticking together. With richly sauced dishes, brown rice can be served perfectly plain and still be tasty. Plain boiled rice can be quickly fried or made into salads to provide an interesting accompaniment to plainer dishes. For a richer rice dish, simmer it gently in just enough water or stock to be absorbed with added herbs and spices to match the main dish.

Even the traditional British grains can be cooked whole. Whole wheat grains, pot barley (the unpolished barley grain), and oat groats all make tasty casseroles which can be served with pulses or other main course dishes.

Another wheat product is burghul, tiny yellow-brown pieces of grain, a product of the Middle East which is the nearest thing to a wholefood convenience food. It consists of whole wheat grains which have been soaked and then cooked at a very high temperature to make them crack. These you can serve cold or hot. To serve cold, soak them in warm water for 30 minutes, drain and squeeze dry with your fingers. Then mix in a vinaigrette dressing plus chopped parsley and any available salad vegetables. It makes a delicious accompaniment and, with a few nuts or pieces of diced cheese or meat or a handful of beans added, can be turned into a main meal. Burghul can also be cooked quickly and served hot as in the recipe on page 86.

Buckwheat consists of tiny, dark brown, heart-shaped seeds which are often used to make the favourite Russian dish known as kasha. It has a distinct, almost pungent, nutty flavour and should be cooked plainly (see page 135) for the first time so you can become accustomed to it. Some people love buckwheat, others cannot get on with it at all. My advice is try it and see. It is delicious with game and all dishes containing pulses.

Millet (yes, the same millet that you give to the budgie!) is a tiny, pale yellow grain that is always served hot. It has a delicate flavour and light fluffy texture, so make it go with casserole dishes or any that have a large amount of gravy or sauce to be soaked up.

Polenta is a traditional Italian food made with cornmeal. This is a yellow-coloured flour produced by grinding up whole, dried sweetcorn kernels (not cornflour, a fine white powder used as a thickener). Polenta is made in a similar way to porridge, with lightly salted water (see page 137). Once made it looks rather heavy and stodgy, but in fact it is extremely light in both texture and flavour. Plain polenta can be served as a side dish and is particularly good with dishes that have a good deal of rich sauce. With a light topping it can become a lunch dish and with a generous topping, polenta will make a substantial main meal. In Italy, polenta is sometimes served as a first course, but remember that it is quite filling and so is best followed by a light salad or perhaps a soup meal.

Another Italian speciality is pasta. I think our wholewheat varieties are delicious. Anything that you can make with white pasta you can make with wholewheat, and it will have a better flavour and texture. Not so long ago all you could buy was wholewheat spaghetti; now you can buy tagliatelle, lasagne, pasta rings and shells and macaroni. None of these takes any longer to cook than white pasta (12 to 20 minutes depending on the type) and you can serve them plain, coated with grated Parmesan cheese or with a small amount of sauce.

Most wholefood shops sell buckwheat spaghetti which is made with a mixture of buckwheat flour and the usual hard durum wheat. It has a very light buckwheat flavour and the added advantage of cooking in 8 to 10 minutes.

Brown Rice with Green Peppers

> 8 oz (225 g) brown rice (short or long grain)
> 2 green peppers
> 3 tbsp oil
> 2 medium onions, finely chopped
> 1 clove garlic, finely chopped
> juice ½ lemon

Simmer the rice in lightly salted water for 45 minutes or until tender. Drain, run cold water through it and drain again. Core, seed and chop the peppers.

Heat the oil in a frying pan over a low heat. Add the onion and garlic and cook until the onion is just beginning to brown. Raise the heat to moderate and fork in the rice and peppers. Heat them through and pour in the lemon juice.

Mix everything together well before taking the pan from the heat.

Brown Rice with Orange

> 8 oz (225 g) brown rice (short or long grain)
> 1 large orange
> 4 tbsp olive oil
> 1 large onion, thinly sliced
> 1 large clove garlic, finely chopped
> 2 tbsp chopped parsley

Simmer the rice in lightly salted water until it is just tender, about 45 minutes. Drain, run cold water through it and drain again.

Grate the rind from the orange. Cut the orange in half crossways and cut away all the remaining pith. Cut each half into lengthways quarters and slice thinly.

Heat the oil in a large heavy frying pan over a low heat. Add the onion and garlic and cook until the onion is golden. Raise the heat and fork in the rice. Allow it to heat through, then mix in the orange rind, sliced orange and parsley. Heat through again quickly and serve immediately.

Turmeric Rice with Mushrooms and Watercress

> 8 oz (225 g) open mushrooms
> 4 tbsp oil
> 1 clove garlic, finely chopped
> 2 tsp ground turmeric
> 1 tsp ground cardamom
> 8 oz (225 g) long grain brown rice
> 1 pint (575 ml) stock
> ¼ tsp sea salt
> 1 bunch watercress

Thinly slice the mushrooms. Heat the oil in a saucepan over a low heat. Stir in the mushrooms, garlic, turmeric and cardamom. Cook gently, stirring frequently, until the juices begin to run from the mushrooms – about 2 minutes. Stir in the rice and cook it for 1 minute. Pour in the stock and bring to the boil. Add the salt.

Cover the pan and set it on a low heat for 45 minutes.

Turn off the heat. Chop the watercress and mix it into the rice. Cover the pan again and let the rice stand for a further 10 minutes.

Paprika Rice with Tomatoes

> 4 tbsp oil
> 1 medium onion, thinly sliced
> 2 tsp paprika
> 8 oz (225 g) long grain brown rice
> 1 pint (575 ml) stock
> 1 tbsp tomato purée

¼ tsp salt
8 oz (225 g) tomatoes

Heat the oil in a saucepan over a low heat. Add the onion and cook until it is just beginning to brown. Stir in the paprika and cook for ½ minute. Add the rice and stir for 1 minute. Pour in the stock and bring to the boil. Add the tomato purée and salt. Cover the pan tightly and set it over a low heat. Cook the rice for 45 minutes, without lifting the lid.

While the rice is cooking, scald, skin and chop the tomatoes. When the rice has cooked, turn off the heat and mix in the tomatoes. Cover the rice again and leave it for a further 10 minutes.

Brown Rice with Olives and Cheese

8 oz (225 g) brown rice (short or long grain)
4 tbsp olive oil
1 medium onion, finely chopped
1 clove garlic, finely chopped
6 green olives, stoned and quartered
2 tbsp grated Parmesan cheese

Simmer the rice in lightly salted water until tender, about 45 minutes. Drain, run cold water through it and drain again.

Heat the oil in a saucepan over a low heat. Add the onion and garlic and soften. Fold in the rice, olives and cheese. Cover the pan and keep it on the low heat for a further 2 minutes.

Brown Rice with Apples and Rosemary

8 oz (225 g) brown rice (short or long grain)
1 large Bramley apple, weighing about 6 oz (175 g)
4 tbsp oil
1 medium onion, thinly sliced
1 clove garlic, finely chopped
2 tsp finely chopped rosemary

Simmer the rice in lightly salted water until tender, about 45 minutes. Drain, run cold water through it and drain again. Quarter, core and thinly slice the apple.

Heat the oil in a saucepan over a low heat. Stir in the apple, onion, garlic and rosemary and cook until the apple and onion are soft. Fold in the rice, cover the pan and keep it on the heat for 2 minutes so the rice just heats through.

Rice, Pineapple and Corn Salad

This is an attractive yellow and pink salad. Serve it with bean salads or cold meats.

> 8 oz (225 g) long grain brown rice
> ½ small fresh pineapple or 8 oz (225 g) tin
>   pineapple in natural juice, drained
> 1 large orange
> 1 yellow pepper, or green if not available
> 12 oz (350 g) tin sweetcorn
> 4 tbsp oil
> 2 tbsp white wine vinegar
> 2 tbsp pineapple juice
> 2 tsp tomato purée
> ¼ tsp Tabasco sauce
> 1 clove garlic, crushed with a pinch sea salt

Cook the rice in lightly salted boiling water for 45 minutes or until tender. Drain, run cold water through it and allow to cool.

Cut the husk and core from the pineapple. Finely chop the flesh. Cut the rind and pith from the orange. Quarter the flesh lengthways and thinly slice it. Core, seed and chop the pepper. Drain the sweetcorn. Mix all these with the rice.

Beat the remaining ingredients together to make the dressing. Mix it into the salad.

Rice and Orange Salad

This is a light and refreshing salad that goes well with fish.

> 8 oz (225 g) long grain brown rice
> 2 large oranges
> juice ½ large orange
> juice ½ lemon
> 4 tbsp oil
> ½ tsp Dijon mustard
> 1 clove garlic, crushed with a pinch sea salt
> ¼ tsp Tabasco sauce
> 4 tbsp chopped parsley

Cook the rice in lightly salted boiling water for 45 minutes or until tender. Drain, run cold water through it and drain again.

Cut the rind and pith from the orange. Cut the flesh into lengthways quarters and thinly slice it. Add to the rice. Beat together the orange and lemon juices, oil, mustard, garlic and Tabasco sauce. Fold the resulting dressing into the salad. Mix in the parsley.

Barley and Mushroom Casserole

> 4 oz (125 g) open mushrooms
> 1 large carrot
> 2 celery sticks
> 1 large onion
> 2 tbsp oil
> 8 oz (225 g) pot barley
> 1 pint (575 ml) stock
> 2 tbsp Worcestershire sauce
> 4 tbsp chopped parsley

Preheat the oven to 350°F (180°C/gas 4). Thinly slice the mushrooms. Finely chop the carrot, celery and onion. Heat the oil in a flameproof casserole dish over a low heat. Add the carrot, celery and onion. Cover and cook them gently for 5 minutes.

Stir in the barley and mushrooms. Pour in the stock and bring to the boil. Add the Worcestershire sauce and parsley.

Cover the casserole and cook in the oven for 45 minutes or until the barley is tender and all the stock has been absorbed.

Wheat and Vegetable Casserole

> 8 oz (225 g) wheat grains
> 8 oz (225 g) aubergine
> 1 tbsp sea salt
> 1 red pepper
> 1 green pepper
> 1 large onion
> 3 tbsp oil
> 1 clove garlic, finely chopped
> 1 tsp paprika
> pinch cayenne pepper
> 1 fl oz (25 ml) stock
> 2 tbsp tomato purée
> 3 tbsp chopped parsley
> 1 tbsp chopped thyme

Boil the wheat grains in lightly salted water for 1 hour. Drain. They should be softened and rounded.

Preheat the oven to 400°F (200°C/gas 6). Halve the aubergine lengthways. Cut the halves into ⅜ inch (1 cm) slices. Put them into a colander, sprinkle with sea salt and leave them to drain for 30 minutes. Rinse them under cold water and dry with kitchen paper.

Core and seed the peppers and cut them into 1 inch (2.5 cm) strips. Thinly slice the onion. Heat the oil in a flameproof casserole dish over a low heat. Add the onion and garlic and soften. Stir in the paprika, cayenne pepper, peppers and aubergine. Mix in the wheat.

Mix together the stock and tomato purée. Pour them into the casserole and bring to the boil. Add the herbs. Cover the casserole and cook in the oven for 30 minutes.

Burghul and Orange Salad

6 oz (175 g) burghul wheat
2 medium oranges
2 tbsp chopped mint
2 tbsp chopped chives
1 tbsp chopped lemon thyme, or common thyme
4 tbsp olive oil
juice ½ lemon
1 clove garlic, crushed with a pinch sea salt
freshly ground black pepper

Soak the wheat in cold water for 30 minutes. Drain and squeeze it dry. Put it into a bowl with the grated rind of one of the oranges. Cut the rind from the other orange and the pith from both. Cut the oranges into lengthways quarters and thinly slice them. Mix them into the wheat with the herbs.

Beat the oil, lemon juice, garlic and pepper together and fold them into the wheat and oranges. Allow to stand for 15 minutes before serving.

Burghul, Olive and Parsley Salad

8 oz (225 g) burghul wheat
20 green olives, stoned and quartered
2 oz (50 g) parsley, chopped
1 small onion, finely chopped
4 tbsp olive oil
1 lemon
sea salt and freshly ground black pepper

Soak the wheat in warm water for 30 minutes. Drain and squeeze it dry. Mix it with the olives, parsley and onion.

Beat together the oil and the juice of half the lemon. Season and mix them with the wheat.

Put the salad into a serving dish. Thinly slice the remaining half lemon. Make the slices into twists and use them as a garnish.

Burghul and Sweetcorn Salad

> 8 oz (225 g) burghul wheat
> 1 red pepper
> 1 green pepper
> 12 oz (350 g) tin sweetcorn
> 4 tbsp sunflower oil
> 2 tbsp white wine vinegar
> 1 tbsp tomato purée
> 1 tsp paprika

Soak the wheat in warm water for 30 minutes. Drain and squeeze it dry.

Core, seed and finely chop the peppers. Drain the sweetcorn. Mix together the wheat, corn and peppers.

Beat the remaining ingredients together to make a dressing and fold it into the salad.

Burghul, Chicory and Avocado Salad

> 8 oz (225 g) burghul wheat
> 4 oz (125 g) chicory
> 1 ripe avocado
> 3 celery sticks
> 8 oz (225 g) tomatoes
> 4 tbsp chopped parsley
> 2 oz (50 g) peanuts (optional)
> 4 tbsp olive oil
> 2 tbsp white wine vinegar
> 1 clove garlic, crushed with a pinch sea salt
> pinch cayenne pepper

Soak the wheat in warm water for 30 minutes. Drain and squeeze it dry.

Halve the chicory lengthways and thinly slice it. Peel, stone and finely chop the avocado. Chop the celery and the tomatoes. Mix these into the wheat together with the parsley and peanuts.

Beat the remaining ingredients together to make the dressing and mix it into the salad.

Olive and Burghul Salad

> 8 oz (225 g) burghul wheat
> 4 tbsp olive oil
> juice ½ lemon
> 2 tbsp tomato purée
> 1 clove garlic, crushed with a pinch sea salt
> freshly ground black pepper
> 12 black olives
> 4 tbsp chopped parsley

Soak the burghul in warm water for 30 minutes. Drain and squeeze it dry. Beat together the oil, lemon juice, tomato purée, garlic and pepper and mix them into the burghul.

Stone and quarter the olives and add them to the burghul with the parsley. Allow to stand for 15 minutes before serving.

Plain Kasha

> 8 oz (225 g) buckwheat groats
> pinch sea salt (optional)

Heat a heavy frying pan over a moderate heat without fat. Put in the buckwheat and stir until it browns. Pour in 1 pint (575 ml) of boiling water. Lower the heat. Cover and simmer for 20 minutes or until the kasha is soft and fluffy and all the water has been absorbed.

Kasha with Egg

> 8 oz (225 g) buckwheat groats
> 1 egg, beaten
> 1 pint (575 ml) stock, or water
> pinch sea salt (optional)

Put the buckwheat into a frying pan and set it on a moderate heat. Stir until it begins to brown. Pour in the egg and quickly stir so it sets round the grains. Pour in the stock or water and bring to the boil. Cover and cook gently for 15 minutes, or until the buckwheat is soft and fluffy.

Kasha with Mushrooms and Green Pepper

This is good with spiced vegetables and pulses and with plain meats.

> 8 oz (225 g) buckwheat groats
> 1 egg, beaten
> 1 pint (575 ml) stock
> 4 oz (125 g) mushrooms, finely chopped
> 1 large or 2 small peppers, cored, seeded and chopped
> 1 medium onion, finely chopped

Put the buckwheat groats into a frying pan and set them over a moderate heat. Stir until they begin to brown. Pour in the egg and stir quickly so it sets around the grains. Pour in the stock and bring to the boil.

Add the mushrooms, pepper and onion. Cover and cook gently for 15 minutes, or until the buckwheat is soft and fluffy.

Sweet-and-sour Millet with Celery

> 4 large celery sticks
> 1 large onion
> 3 tbsp oil
> 1 clove garlic, finely chopped
> 1 pint (575 ml) stock
> 2 tbsp tamari sauce
> 2 tsp tomato purée
> 1 tbsp white wine vinegar
> 8 oz (225 g) millet

Finely chop the celery sticks and onion. Heat the oil in a frying pan over a low heat. Put in the celery, onion and garlic and cook, stirring occasionally, until they begin to turn golden. In the meantime, mix together the stock, tamari sauce, tomato purée and vinegar.

Stir the millet into the pan and keep stirring for 1 minute. Pour in the stock and bring to the boil. Cover and simmer for 20 minutes or until the millet is soft and fluffy and all the stock has been absorbed.

Millet with Tomatoes

This dish is light, fluffy and moist, red in colour and has a tomato flavour.

> 8 oz (225 g) tomatoes
> 3 tbsp oil
> 1 large onion, finely chopped
> 1 clove garlic, finely chopped
> 8 oz (225 g) millet
> 1 tsp ground paprika
> ¼ pint (150 ml) tomato juice
> ¾ pint (425 ml) stock

Scald, skin and chop the tomatoes. Heat the oil in a frying pan over a low heat. Add the onion and garlic and soften. Stir in the millet and paprika and cook for 1 minute. Pour in the stock and tomato juice and bring to the boil. Add the tomatoes. Cover and simmer for 20 minutes or until the millet is soft and fluffy and all the liquid has been absorbed.

Alternative: add a cored, seeded and chopped green pepper when softening the onions.

Polenta, Basic Recipe

> ¼ tsp sea salt
> 5 oz (150 g) cornmeal

Put 1½ pints (850 ml) of water into a saucepan and bring it to the boil. Add the salt and turn the heat down a little so the water is just simmering. Pour the polenta into the water in a thin, slow stream, stirring all the time with a wooden spoon. Keep stirring for about 20 minutes or until the 'porridge' is thick and pulls away from the sides of the pan as you stir. Take the pan from the heat.

Once the polenta is made, you can mix other ingredients, such as grated cheese or softened onion and herbs, into it and serve immediately. It can also be poured into a flat dish and left to cool and set. After this it can be topped with other ingredients and baked or cut into slices and grilled or fried.

Polenta with Peppers and Tomatoes

> 2 green peppers
> 4 small tomatoes
> 4 tbsp olive oil
> 1 medium onion, finely chopped
> 1 clove garlic, finely chopped
> 1 tbsp chopped parsley
> ½ tbsp chopped thyme
> ½ tbsp chopped marjoram
> 1 quantity basic recipe polenta (see page 137)

Core, seed and finely chop the peppers. Scald, skin and finely chop the tomatoes. Heat the oil in a frying pan over a low heat. Add the peppers, onion, garlic and herbs and cook until the onion is soft. Mix in the tomatoes and take the pan from the heat.

Mix all the contents of the pan into the cooked polenta. Turn out into a warm serving dish. This polenta is good with casseroles, particularly those containing beef or lamb. It also goes well with offal and with cheese.

Spaghetti with Yoghurt and Parmesan

A creamy but light sauce with a good cheesy flavour.

> 8 oz (225 g) wholewheat spaghetti
> ¼ pint (150 ml) natural yoghurt

  1 oz (25 g) Parmesan cheese, grated
  4 tbsp chopped parsley
  1 clove garlic, crushed with a pinch sea salt
  freshly ground black pepper

Cook the spaghetti in lightly salted water for 12 minutes or until tender. Drain, run warm water through it and drain again. Return it to the saucepan.

   Beat together the yoghurt, cheese, parsley, garlic and pepper. Carefully fold into the spaghetti. Set the pan over a low heat and gently warm the spaghetti through, taking care that the yoghurt doesn't boil and curdle.

Spaghetti with Sage and Tomato Coating

This is not a thick or runny sauce but a light, flavoured coating.

  ¼ pint (150 ml) tomato juice
  1 tbsp arrowroot
  1½ tsp dried sage
  1 clove garlic, crushed with a pinch sea salt
  8 oz (225 g) wholewheat spaghetti, cooked until
     tender, drained

Mix 4 tbsp of the tomato juice with the arrowroot. Put the rest into a saucepan with the garlic and sage. Bring it to the boil. Stir in the arrowroot mixture and stir over a low heat until thick. Remove the pan from the heat and gently fold in the cooked spaghetti.

Tagliatelle with Peanut and Orange Sauce

This light sauce with a good nutty flavour coats the tagliatelle well.

  8 oz (225 g) tagliatelle
  juice 1 large orange
  2 tbsp oil
  2 tbsp crunchy peanut butter

2 tbsp tomato purée
1 clove garlic, crushed with a pinch sea salt
freshly ground black pepper

Boil the tagliatelle in lightly salted water for 10 minutes or until tender. Drain and run cold water through it.

Put all the remaining ingredients into a saucepan and stir well to mix thoroughly. Set them over a medium heat and bring to just below boiling. Gently fold in the tagliatelle and stir to heat through.

Avocado Pasta

8 oz (225 g) wholewheat pasta shells
1 ripe avocado
2 tbsp olive oil
juice ½ lemon
1 clove garlic, crushed with a pinch sea salt
4 tbsp chopped parsley
freshly ground black pepper

Cook the pasta in lightly salted boiling water until just tender, about 10 minutes. Drain and steam it dry.

While the pasta is cooking, peel, stone and mash the avocado and mix in the oil, lemon juice, garlic, parsley and pepper. Put the avocado sauce into a saucepan and heat it gently. Stir in the drained pasta and heat through if necessary.

Buckwheat Spaghetti with Yoghurt and Paprika

8 oz (225 g) buckwheat spaghetti
4 tbsp natural yoghurt
2 tsp paprika

Cook the spaghetti in lightly salted water for 8 to 10 minutes or until tender. Drain, refresh and drain again.

Put the yoghurt and paprika together in the saucepan and

gently warm them. Fold in the spaghetti, make sure it warms through, and serve immediately.

Tomato Sauce for Pasta

This is good for all types of pasta: spoon it on top of spaghetti and tagliatelle, fold it into pasta shells and rings. It can be topped with grated Parmesan cheese for extra flavour.

> 1 lb (450 g) tomatoes
> 2 tbsp oil
> 1 medium onion, finely chopped
> 1 clove garlic, finely chopped
> 1 tbsp tomato purée
> 1 tsp dried mixed herbs

Scald, skin and finely chop the tomatoes. Heat the oil in a saucepan over a low heat. Add the onion and garlic and soften. Add the tomatoes, tomato purée and herbs. Simmer, uncovered, for 10 minutes or until the tomatoes are soft and make a thick sauce.

Pasta, Tomato and Black Olive Salad

> 8 oz (225 g) wholewheat pasta shells or rings
> 1 lb (450 g) tomatoes
> 10 black olives
> 2 tbsp chopped thyme
> 4 tbsp olive oil
> 2 tbsp white wine vinegar
> 1 clove garlic, crushed with a pinch sea salt
> ½ tsp paprika
> pinch cayenne pepper

Cook the pasta in lightly salted water until tender, about 10 minutes. Drain, run cold water through it and drain again. If you are using pasta shells, make sure that they have drained properly.

Finely chop the tomatoes. Stone and quarter the olives. Put

them into a bowl with the pasta. Beat the remaining ingredients together and mix them into the salad.

Tagliatelle and Green Olive Salad

> 8 oz (225 g) wholewheat tagliatelle
> 20 green olives
> 6 tbsp olive oil
> 1 clove garlic, crushed with a pinch sea salt
> freshly ground black pepper
> 6 tbsp chopped parsley
> 1 tbsp chopped basil, if available
> 2 tbsp chopped capers

Boil the tagliatelle in lightly salted boiling water until tender, about 10 minutes. Drain, run cold water through it and drain again. Stone and finely chop the olives.

In a bowl, mix together the oil, garlic and pepper. Fold in the tagliatelle and leave it until it is completely cold. Add the olives, herbs and capers.

Desserts

Eating wholefoods does not mean that you have to give up sweet things after a meal. It is just a question of choosing the right sweet things. A rich mousse, for example, full of double cream and white sugar could in no way be called healthy, but make one with natural yoghurt and sweeten it with natural fruit juice and perhaps a little honey, and it is quite a different story.

The simplest of all desserts is fresh fruit. Besides being naturally sweet fruit is an excellent source of vitamin C, some B vitamins and fibre. Yellow-coloured fruits contain vitamin A and the citrus fruits vitamin K.

After informal family meals, you can simply put a bowl of several varieties of fresh fruit on the table plus, if you like, small bowls of dried fruits and mixed nuts.

Fresh fruits can also be made into a wide variety of fruit salads, which can change their ingredients according to the season. Use four or more fruits in any mixture. Chop the larger ones such as apples and pears into small, even-sized pieces. Leave very small ones such as raspberries or seedless grapes whole, and halve or slice the medium-sized ones such as strawberries and plums. I prefer the fruit without any added sweetener, enjoying the contrast between the sweet and the slightly sharp. If you find that your tooth is still too sweet for this, trickle over a little melted and cooled honey and then leave the fruit to stand for at least 30 minutes to allow the natural juices to combine with it.

A small portion of whipped or double cream as an occasional treat will do a healthy person no harm, but it is best not to have it every day. Instead, top a fruit salad with natural yoghurt or a low fat soft cheese such as quark and on top of this sprinkle over small amounts of chopped nuts, a crunchy oat cereal, sesame or sunflower seeds, or a very tiny amount of finely grated carob bar. My favourite topping is made by soaking desiccated coconut in natural yoghurt for about 4 hours to make it soft. This results in a delicious combination of sweet, nutty and sharp flavours.

The same coconut mixture makes an ideal topping for soaked dried fruits. These are exceptionally sweet and need no added sweeteners. The best way to prepare them is to soak them in natural fruit juice for 8 hours or overnight. They can be served as they are, mixed with fresh fruits such as diced pineapple or orange slices, or gently heated, before serving, with a slice of lemon and a cinnamon stick. Serve them with the same toppings as for fresh fruits.

These are all easy, no-cook sweets. If you fancy a simple cooked sweet, try grilling fruits, baking apples and steaming pears. For special occasions, use cooked fruit as a base for light mousses, pies and tarts. You can cut down on the final amount of sweetener that you use by cooking them with dried fruits or in sweet natural fruit juice such as pineapple or orange juice. My latest discovery is prune juice which is dark, rich and sweet and ideal for cooking. If you drink it, it is best to dilute it with mineral water. Where the recipes mention gelatin, I mean leaf gelatin, which I recommend if you can get hold of it.

Another fairly new item to be welcomed on to the supermarket shelf is fruit tinned in natural fruit juice. It makes an excellent stand-by in the store-cupboard and can be served just as it is as part of a more complicated dessert.

At the end of this chapter I have included three Christmas specials. I could never understand why recipes for mincemeat and Christmas pudding always contain so much sugar, since they are packed with dried fruits which provide more than enough sweetness. On experimenting, I found that with careful blending of other ingredients the sugar was indeed unnecessary. The mincemeat is rich and fruity. I like to pack it into a large double-crust tart, besides making small mince pies. The Christmas jelly pudding makes a light end to the Christmas meal while still containing the traditional ingredients and looking very much as a pudding should. The final recipe is my own particular favourite Christmas pudding. Over the years I have added things and taken away others and this is the final result. Don't be afraid of the carrot: it doesn't show and doesn't taste but simply adds a rich sweetness. One word of warning: this type of sugar-free pudding does not keep for longer than a month so make it some time in late November.

Tropical Fruit Salad

 2 mangoes
 4 kiwi fruits
 8 fresh dates
 ¼ pint (150 ml) natural yoghurt
 freshly grated nutmeg
 2 pieces preserved stem ginger, finely chopped
 4 walnut halves to garnish

To prepare the mangoes, cut a thick slice from each flat side. Scoop out and chop the flesh from the slices. Cut away the skin from the remaining pieces. Cut away the flesh from the stone and chop it. Divide the chopped mango between 4 small plates, piling it in the centre.

Peel the kiwi fruit and cut each one into 4 slices. Arrange the slices round the mango. Halve and stone the dates and arrange the halves between the kiwi slices.

Spoon the yoghurt over the mango only. Grate on a little nutmeg and scatter the chopped ginger over it. Top with a walnut half.

Stuffed Apple and Banana Salad

Serve this as an unusual combination of sweet and cheese.

 4 large eating apples
 2 ripe bananas
 4 oz (125 g) curd cheese
 1 tbsp cider vinegar
 4 hazelnuts to garnish

Stand the apples on their stalk ends. Cut a ¼ inch (6 mm) slice off the top of each one. Chop the edible part of the tops finely and discard the centre core. If the apples don't stand up properly, take a slice off the bottom. Using a small teaspoon, scoop out as much of the middles of the apples as possible, leaving shells about ⅛ inch (3 mm) thick. Discard the core and chop the rest.

Mash the bananas and mix them with the cheese. Add the vinegar and mix well. Stir in the chopped apple.

Put the mixture into the apple shells. It will pile up quite high. Top with a hazelnut.

Dried Fruit Snow

> 8 oz (225 g) dried mixed fruits (prunes, apples, whole apricots, peaches, pears)
> ¾ pint (425 ml) natural orange juice
> ½ pint (275 ml) natural yoghurt
> 2 oz (50 g) desiccated coconut

Soak the fruits in the orange juice for at least 8 hours. Soak the coconut in the yoghurt. Spoon the fruits into individual dishes and spoon the yoghurt and coconut mixture over the top.

Summer Fruit Bowl

This is a delicious, dark red, glossy, mixture of summer fruits which is refreshing and not heavy. The ideal summer sweet.

> 4 oz (125 g) redcurrants
> 8 oz (225 g) blackcurrants
> 2 oz (50 g) honey, or more to taste
> 1 tbsp arrowroot
> 4 oz (100 g) strawberries
> 6 oz (175 g) red or black cherries
> 4 oz (100 g) raspberries
> whipped cream, soured cream or natural yoghurt, to serve

String the red- and blackcurrants. Put them into a saucepan with 4 tbsp water. Cover and set over a low heat for 10 minutes or until the fruit is very juicy. Rub through a sieve.

Return all the purée but 2 tbsp to the cleaned pan. Add the honey and stir over a low heat until it dissolves. Stir the arrowroot into the remaining fruit purée and stir the mixture into the saucepan. Bring the purée to the boil, stirring until it thickens. Turn it into a bowl and allow it to cool.

Hull the strawberries and halve or quarter them if they are large. Stone the cherries.

Mix the strawberries, cherries and raspberries into the thickened fruit purée. Chill before serving. Serve with whipped cream, soured cream or natural yoghurt.

Grilled Orange Slices

> 2 oz (50 g) sultanas
> ¼ pint (150 ml) natural orange juice
> 4 tbsp whisky or tequila (optional)
> 4 large Spanish oranges
> 2 oz (50 g) honey
> ¼ tsp ground cinnamon

Soak the sultanas in the orange juice and spirit for four hours. Place in a saucepan and bring to just below boiling point and keep warm.

Cut the rind and pith from the oranges. Cut the flesh into ¼ inch (6 mm) slices. Lay them on a large, flat flameproof dish, overlapping as little as possible.

Put the honey and cinnamon into a saucepan and set over a low heat for the honey to melt. Pour evenly over the oranges.

Heat the grill to high. Put the dish under the grill so the oranges are about 4 inches (10 cm) from the heat. Grill for 3 minutes, without turning, so they brown. Drain the sultanas and scatter them over the top. Serve straight from the dish.

Grilled Apple Slices with Clove Honey

> 4 medium cooking apples
> 1 oz (25 g) butter
> 3 tbsp honey
> ½ tsp ground cloves
> natural yoghurt, to serve

Peel and core the apples. Cut them into ¼ inch (6 mm) thick rings. Arrange them in a shallow heatproof dish, overlapping as little as possible. Melt the butter in a saucepan over a low heat and remove it before it foams. Brush the butter over the apples. Put the honey into a saucepan with the ground cloves and melt it over a low heat. Spoon over the apples.

Heat the grill to high. Put the dish under the grill so that the apple rings are about 2 inches (5 cm) from the heat. Cook until they are brown and bubbling on both sides, turning once. Serve from the dish and hand the yoghurt separately.

Banana and Apricot Kebabs

4 bananas
12 fresh apricots
2 oz (50 g) honey
1 tsp ground cinnamon

Cut each banana into 6 pieces. Halve and stone the apricots. Thread them alternately on 4 kebab skewers. Put the honey and cinnamon into a small pan and set them over a low heat (it is best to cook this indoors) until the honey melts. Brush the spiced honey over the kebabs.

Grill the kebabs under a medium grill for about 7 minutes, turning them several times. The bananas should just be beginning to brown.

Bananas in Marsala

Sultanas and marsala make a rich, sweet sauce for baked bananas.

6 bananas
2 oz (50 g) sultanas
grated rind and juice 1 medium orange
6 tbsp marsala
butter for greasing
yoghurt or soured cream, to serve

Preheat the oven to 400°F (200°C/gas 6). Slice the bananas into ¼ inch (6 mm) thick rounds and mix them in a small pie dish with the sultanas and orange rind. Pour in the orange juice and marsala and cover the dish with lightly buttered foil.

Bake the bananas for 20 minutes and serve them hot with yoghurt or soured cream.

Steamed Comice Pears

> 4 firm comice pears
> 2 oz (50 g) sultanas
> 2 oz (50 g) blanched almonds
> ½ tsp ground cinnamon
> pinch ground mace
> 2 tbsp honey

Cut 1 inch (2.5 cm) tops from the pears, leaving the stalks intact. Core the pears. Finely chop or mince the sultanas and almonds. Mix them with the spices and honey. Fill the pears with the mixture. Replace the tops and anchor them with toothpicks.

Set the pears upright in a heatproof plate or dish. Place the dish in a steamer and the steamer in a large pan of boiling water. Cook the pears over gently boiling water for 30 minutes or until tender.

Strawberry and Raspberry Mould

This is a pretty and light summer sweet.

> 1 lb (450 g) cottage cheese
> 2 tbsp honey
> 8 oz (225 g) strawberries
> 2 oz (450 g) ripe raspberries
> mint leaves, to decorate

Rub the cottage cheese through a sieve and beat in the honey so it becomes well incorporated. Hull the strawberries and quarter half of them. Fold the raspberries into the cheese, bruising them slightly so the cheese becomes marbled with pink. Carefully fold in the quartered strawberries. Put the mixture into a lightly oiled pudding basin and smooth the top. Chill it for 1 hour.

Turn the mould out on to a plate. It will be slightly rounded rather than pudding-basin shaped. Smooth the surface with a rounded knife. Halve the remaining strawberries and press them into the sides of the mould as a decoration. Decorate the edges of the plate with mint leaves.

Pashka

Pashka is a Russian dish traditionally served at Easter. It usually contains butter and cream. This is much lighter but still retains the authentic flavour of the original.

> 12 oz (350 g) curd cheese
> 3 tbsp natural yoghurt
> 4 oz (125 g) almonds
> 4 oz (125 g) glacé cherries
> 2 oz (50 g) candied peel
> 2 oz (50 g) dried apricots

Beat the curd cheese to a cream and beat in the yoghurt. Blanch and grind the almonds. Quarter the cherries. Finely chop the candied peel and apricots. Mix them all into the cheese.

Put the mixture into a 1 pint (575 ml) oiled pudding basin and chill for 2 hours. Turn it out on to a plate for serving. The pashka can be garnished, if wished, with more nuts and fruits.

Gooseberry Water Ice

> 1 lb (450 g) gooseberries
> ½ pint (275 ml) white grape juice
> 2 tbsp honey
> 3 oz (75 g) light Barbados sugar

Top and tail the gooseberries. Put them into a saucepan with the grape juice and honey. Cover and set over a low heat for 15 minutes or until the fruit is very soft.

Put ½ pint (275 ml) water and the sugar into a saucepan. Set over a low heat and stir until the sugar has dissolved. Boil for 5 minutes. Stir the syrup into the gooseberry purée.

Cool the mixture and then chill it. Pour it into a freezing tray. Turn the freezer or the refrigerator to the lowest temperature and freeze it to a slush, about 2 hours. Take it out and whip it well to break up the ice crystals. Freeze it for a further hour and whip it again.

Pack the water ice in a lidded plastic container and freeze completely.

It will keep for up to a month in the freezer or up to a week in the freezing compartment of the refrigerator.

Peach Yoghurt Ice

    2 peaches
    2 egg yolks
    2 oz (50 g) honey
    1 pint (575 ml) natural yoghurt

Scald, skin and dice the peaches. Either sieve them or work them to a purée in a liquidizer or food processor.

Whip the egg yolks until they begin to froth. Put the honey into a saucepan and bring it to just below boiling point. Whip it into the egg yolks and continue to whip until the mixture is light and fluffy. Beat in the yoghurt and peach purée. Pour the mixture into a freezing tray.

Turn the refrigerator or freezer to the lowest temperature and freeze the mixture to a slush, about 2 hours. Take it out and whip it well. Freeze it for another 2 hours and whip it again. Pack the ice-cream in a lidded plastic container and freeze completely.

Before serving, take it into room temperature for about 30 minutes.

The ice-cream will keep for up to 2 months in the freezer or up to 2 weeks in the freezing compartment of the refrigerator.

Mango Ice

2 ripe mangoes
juice 1 lime
1 egg white
candied peel, or angelica, to decorate (optional)

Cut a thick slice from each flat side of the mango. Scoop out the flesh. Cut the skin from the remaining piece and cut the flesh away from the stone.

Either mash the mango flesh well or liquidize it. Add the lime juice and mix well.

Put the mango into a freezing tray and put the tray into the freezer or into the freezing compartment of the refrigerator, set at the lowest temperature. Freeze for 2 hours.

Stiffly whip the egg white. Whip the frozen mangoes. Fold them into the egg white. Return the mixture to the freezing tray. Freeze for 2 hours, whipping well after the first hour.

Serve in chilled glasses, decorated with chopped candied peel or angelica.

Maple Syrup Ice-cream

This is a delicious, rich tasting ice-cream. These amounts will serve 8.

½ pint (275 ml) double cream
½ pint (275 ml) natural yoghurt
4 tbsp maple syrup
¼ tsp sea salt

To serve
2 to 3 tbsp maple syrup
1 tbsp chopped walnuts per portion
1 fresh peach or 3 oz (75 g) puréed apple per portion

Whip the cream until it thickens slightly. Then whip in the yoghurt so the mixture becomes light and fluffy. Whip in the maple syrup and salt. Put the mixture into a bowl and put it into the freezer or the freezing compartment of a refrigerator set at its lowest temperature. Freeze it until it is slushy. Take it out and whip the mixture so it becomes fluffy and smooth again.

Freeze the ice-cream again for 4 hours. Either scoop it out and serve it straight away or whip it again and put it into a lidded plastic container and keep it in the freezer or in the freezing compartment of a refrigerator at a normal setting.

To serve: if you are using peaches, cut them into quarters and stone them. Arrange the quarters in a star shape on dishes. Or, simply put a portion of puréed apple into the dishes. Scoop the ice-cream on top. Heat the maple syrup so it is hot but not boiling and pour it over the ice-cream. Scatter the chopped nuts over the top and serve immediately.

Peach Melba Jellies

> 4 peaches
> ½ oz (15 g) gelatin
> 8 oz (225 g) raspberries
> ¼ pint (150 ml) red wine
> 1 oz (25 g) light Barbados sugar
> 2 oz (50 g) low fat soft cheese
> 4 tbsp double cream

Scald, skin and dice the peaches and divide them between 4 small glass dishes. In a small pan, soak the gelatin in 4 tbsp warm water.

Put all but four of the raspberries into a saucepan with the wine. Cover and set over a low heat for 10 minutes or until the fruit is soft and very juicy. Rub through a sieve. Return them to the cleaned pan and add the sugar. Stir over a low heat until it dissolves. Gently melt the gelatin and stir it into the raspberry purée. Leave the purée to cool completely.

When it is cool but still liquid, pour it over the peaches. Leave the jellies in a cool place to set.

Beat together the cheese and cream. Top each jelly with a portion of the mixture and garnish with the remaining raspberries.

Apricot and Orange Jelly

This is a sweet, rich jelly packed full of apricots.

        8 oz (225 g) dried whole apricots, halved lengthways
        3 large oranges
        ¾ pint (425 ml) apple juice
        ½ oz (15 g) gelatin
        natural yoghurt or soured cream, to serve (optional)

Put the apricots into a saucepan. Thinly pare the rind of one orange and cut it into small, thin slivers. Squeeze the juice. Add the rind to the apricots and pour in the apple juice. Set the pan over a low heat and bring to the boil. Simmer for 10 minutes. Remove the pan from the heat. Add the orange juice. Leave to cool for about 1 hour.

Strain the apricots, reserving the juices and the slivers of orange rind. Oil an 8 inch (20 cm) diameter ring mould. Arrange the orange rind slivers all round the base and put the apricots on top. Soak the gelatin in 4 tbsp of the juice in a small pan for 5 minutes. Melt gently and stir it into the rest of the juice. Pour the juice evenly over the apricots. Put the jelly into the refrigerator for 1 hour to set.

Cut the rind and pith from the remaining oranges. Cut the flesh into lengthways quarters and thinly slice them. Turn the jelly on to a flat plate and fill the centre with the oranges.

Serve yoghurt or soured cream separately if wished.

Blackberry and Yoghurt Mousse

This is a light, fluffy mousse with a refreshing flavour.

        8 oz (225 g) sweet blackberries
        4 fl oz (125 ml) prune juice
        2 tsp honey
        ½ oz (15 g) gelatin
        2 eggs, separated
        ½ pint (275 ml) natural yoghurt

Put the blackberries into a saucepan with the prune juice. Cover them and set them over a low heat until they are soft and juicy – about 10 minutes. Rub them through a sieve. Return them to the saucepan and stir in the honey. Soak the gelatin in 4 tbsp warm water.

Beat the egg yolks one at a time into the blackberry purée. Stir over a low heat until the mixture thickens and coats the back of a wooden spoon. Take the pan from the heat. Melt the gelatin on a low heat. Quickly stir it into the blackberry purée. Leave the mixture in a cool place until it is on the point of setting.

Stiffly whip the egg whites. Fold first the yoghurt and then the egg whites into the blackberry mixture. Pour the mousse into either one large serving bowl or into four individual dishes. Leave it in a cool place to set.

Blackcurrant Cheese Mousse

This can also be made with an 8 oz (225 g) tin of blackcurrants in natural juice. Sieve, add honey to taste, but omit the wine.

> 8 oz (225 g) blackcurrants (see above)
> 2 tbsp honey
> 4 tbsp red wine
> ½ oz (15 g) gelatin
> 2 eggs, separated
> 4 oz (100 g) low fat soft cheese

String the blackcurrants. Put them into a saucepan with the honey and wine. Cover them and set them over a low heat for 10 minutes or until they are soft and juicy. Rub through a sieve. In a small pan, soak the gelatin in 4 tbsp warm water.

Put 1 tbsp of the blackcurrant purée into each of four glass dishes. Return the rest to the cleaned pan and set it over a very low heat. Beat in the egg yolks, one at a time and cook, stirring, without boiling, until the mixture coats the back of a wooden spoon. Melt the gelatin and stir it into the thickened purée. Cool the mixture.

Put the cheese into a bowl and gradually beat in the thickened blackcurrant purée. Stiffly whip the egg whites and fold them into the rest.

Pile the mousse into the glasses. Leave in a cool place to set.

Fluffy Pineapple Custard

This is sweet, light and easy to eat.

8 oz (225 g) tin pineapple rings in natural juice
2 eggs, separated
¼ pint (150 ml) creamy milk
½ oz (15 g) gelatin
2 tbsp crunchy toasted oat cereal, to serve

Liquidize the pineapple together with the juice. Put the egg yolks in a saucepan and add the milk. Stir over a very low heat, making sure the mixture does not boil, until you have a thick custard. Allow to cool slightly.

In a small pan, soak the gelatin in 4 tbsp warm water. Melt it gently over a low heat. Add the custard and the gelatin to the pineapple and liquidize again. Leave the mixture until it is on the point of setting.

Stiffly whip the egg whites and fold them into the rest. Pour the custard either into individual bowls or one large serving dish. Leave in a cool place for 2 hours to set. Sprinkle the toasted cereal over the top just before serving.

Strawberry and Soured Cream Mousse

8 oz (225 g) strawberries
3 drops almond essence
½ oz (15 g) gelatin
juice ½ lemon
2 tbsp honey
2 eggs, separated
¼ pint (150 ml) soured cream
4 oz (125 g) strawberries, to decorate

Rub the strawberries through a sieve or purée them in a blender. Mix in the almond essence. Soak the gelatin in the lemon juice.

Put the strawberries in a saucepan and add the honey. Set

them over a low heat and stir until the honey dissolves. Beat in the egg yolks and stir until the mixture coats the back of a wooden spoon. Gently melt the gelatin and quickly stir it into the strawberries. Take the pan from the heat and leave the strawberries until they are on the point of setting.

Whip the soured cream until it is light and airy (it won't stiffen like double cream). Stiffly whip the egg whites. Fold first the cream and then the egg whites into the strawberry mixture. Pour the mousse into one large glass bowl or into individual dishes. Leave in a cool place to set.

Just before serving, garnish with fresh strawberries.

Rhubarb and Semolina Mousse

Rhubarb and semolina tend to remind one of school dinners, but mixed together in this way they make an attractive, light, fluffy dessert with a mousse-like texture.

> 1 oz (25 g) wholewheat semolina
> ½ pint (275 ml) skimmed milk
> 1 oz (25 g) gelatin
> 1¼ lbs (575 g) rhubarb
> ¼ pint (150 ml) natural apple juice
> 4 oz (125 g) honey
> 2 eggs, separated
> oil for greasing

Put the semolina into a saucepan and stir in the milk. Bring to the boil, stirring, and simmer gently for about 15 minutes or until it thickens, stirring frequently. Take the pan from the heat.

Soak the gelatin in 6 tbsp cold water. Chop the rhubarb and put it in a saucepan with the apple juice. Bring to the boil, cover and simmer for 15 minutes or until the rhubarb is soft. After it has been cooking for 5 minutes, take out and reserve 9 evenly shaped pieces.

Put the cooked rhubarb through the fine blade of a vegetable mill or rub it through a sieve. Stir in the honey. Melt the gelatin over a low heat and stir it into the rhubarb purée. Pour the rhubarb into an oiled 2 pint (1.25 l) charlotte mould to a depth of ¼ inch (6 mm). Arrange the reserved pieces of rhubarb in the bottom. Leave the tin in the refrigerator for the purée to set.

Beat the egg yolks into the semolina and then stir in the remaining rhubarb purée. Cool the mixture until it is on the point of setting.

Stiffly whip the egg whites and fold them into the rhubarb and semolina mixture. Pour the mixture into the mould and leave it for 2 hours in a cool place or in the refrigerator to set.

Turn the mousse on to a flat plate to serve.

Rice and Apple Mould

Sweet dessert apples are all the sweetener necessary for this soft, creamy mould.

> 2 oz (50 g) flaked brown rice
> ¼ nutmeg, grated
> 1 pint (575 ml) skimmed milk
> 3 medium sweet dessert apples (russets are best)
> ¾ pint (425 ml) apple juice
> ½ oz (15 g) gelatin
> oil for greasing

Put the rice into a double saucepan with the nutmeg and milk. Set over a low heat for about 2 hours, stirring frequently, so you have a thick mixture. While the rice is cooking, peel and core the apples and cut them into thin lengthways slices. Poach the apple slices in the apple juice for 10 minutes so they are soft but still in shape. Drain and reserve both apples and juice.

Soak the gelatin in a small pan in 4 tbsp of warm apple juice for 5 minutes. Melt it over a low heat and stir it into the remaining juice. Oil an 8 inch (20 cm) diameter ring mould. Arrange a ring of apple slices in the base and pour in about one-third of the apple jelly. Put the mould into the refrigerator for the jelly to set.

Chop the remaining apples and mix these and the remaining juice into the rice. Spoon the rice mixture on top of the set jelly and put the mould into the refrigerator again until the rice is firm.

Turn the mould on to a plate to serve.

Spicy Apple Cake

    4 medium cooking apples
    4 oz (125 g) wholewheat flour
    ½ tsp bicarbonate of soda
    ½ tsp ground cinnamon
    ½ tsp ground mixed spices
    freshly grated nutmeg
    2 oz (50 g) butter or vegetable margarine plus
        extra for greasing
    2 oz (50 g) honey
    1 egg, beaten
    natural yoghurt, to serve

Preheat the oven to 400°F (200°C/gas 6). Wipe and core two of the apples. Put them into an ovenproof dish and pour in a little water. Bake for 20 minutes or until they are soft. Skin and sieve them. Turn the oven to 350°F (180°C/gas 4).

Mix the flour with the bicarbonate of soda, cinnamon and mixed spices and grate in a little nutmeg. Beat the butter or margarine in a bowl to soften. Beat in the honey and gradually add the egg and then the apple pulp. Beat in the flour and spices.

Peel, core and slice the remaining apples. Arrange them in the base of a greased 7 inch (18 cm) cake tin. Put the cake mixture on top. Bake the cake for 50 minutes or until a skewer inserted in the centre comes out clean.

Turn the cake on to a flat plate and leave it so that the apple rings are on top. Serve hot with natural yoghurt.

Quick Apple and Mincemeat Crumble

This is a good way of using up the last of the Christmas mincemeat. The crumble is easily made but it tastes as though you have gone to tremendous trouble!

    2 really large cooking apples
    8 oz (225 g) healthy mincemeat (see page 164)
    3 oz (75 g) wholewheat bread
    2 oz (50 g) butter or vegetable margarine

Preheat the oven to 400°F (200°C/gas 6). Peel, quarter, core and thinly slice the apples and mix them with the mincemeat. Put them into a 7 or 8 inch (18 or 20 cm) diameter tart dish.

Make the bread into fine crumbs. Melt the butter in a frying pan over a very low heat without letting it bubble or brown. Stir in the breadcrumbs and let them get well coated. Spoon them evenly over the apple mixture and bake for 30 minutes.

Rhubarb and Orange Crumble

> 8 oz (225 g) rhubarb
> 3 medium oranges
> 2 oz (50 g) sultanas
> 2 oz (50 g) demerara sugar
> ¼ tsp ground ginger
> ½ tsp ground cinnamon
> 3 oz (75 g) muesli base
> ½ oz (15 g) wheatgerm
> ½ oz (15 g) chopped, toasted hazelnuts
> 1 oz (25 g) desiccated coconut
> 3 tbsp sunflower oil

Preheat the oven to 375°F (190°C/gas 5). Finely chop the rhubarb. Cut the rind and pith from the oranges. Cut the oranges lengthways into quarters and thinly slice them. Mix the rhubarb and oranges with the sultanas, sugar and spices and put them into a pie dish.

Mix the rest of the ingredients together making sure that the oil coats everything well and pile the mixture on to the rhubarb base making sure it covers it completely.

Bake for 30 minutes and serve hot or cold.

Plum and Almond Layer

> 1½ lb (675 g) cooking plums
> 4 oz (125 g) pressed dates
> 4 oz (125 g) ground almonds
> 2 oz (50 g) sugar-free muesli
> 2 tbsp sunflower oil
> soured cream or natural yoghurt for serving

Preheat the oven to 400°F (200°C/gas 6). Halve and stone the plums. Finely chop the dates. Mix all but 1 oz (25 g) of the ground almonds with the dates. Mix the remaining almonds with the muesli base and oil.

In an ovenproof dish, put one-third of the plums and scatter them with half the almond and date mixture. Put in another third of the plums and then the remaining date mixture. Top with the remaining plums and then the almond and muesli mixture. Bake for 25 minutes or until the top is golden brown.

Cherry Cheesecake

This is a light-textured cheesecake for a special occasion.

8 oz (225 g) red cherries

Base
3 oz (75 g) plain oatcakes
4 oz (125 g) digestive biscuits
3 oz (75 g) butter
½ tsp ground cinnamon
3 drops almond essence

Syrup
1½ oz (40 g) honey
2 inch (5 cm) cinnamon stick
2 drops almond essence
1 tsp arrowroot

Topping
½ oz (15 g) gelatin
juice 1 lemon
6 oz (175 g) curd cheese
2 eggs, separated
2 oz (50 g) honey
¼ pint (150 ml) natural yoghurt

Preheat the oven to 350°F (180°C/gas 4). To make the base, break up the biscuits, sandwich them between two pieces of greaseproof paper and crush them to fine crumbs with a rolling pin. Alternatively, work them in a liquidizer or food processor. Melt the butter in a saucepan over a low heat and stir in the crumbs, cinnamon and almond essence. Press the mixture into the bottom of a 7 inch (18 cm) diameter cake tin with a removable base and bake it for 15 minutes. Allow it to cool completely.

Stone the cherries. Put 6 tbsp water with the honey into a saucepan and stir them over a low heat until the honey dissolves. Bring to the boil and add the cherries, cinnamon stick and almond essence. Gently cook the cherries, covered, for 10 minutes. Remove from the heat, drain and reserve both cherries and syrup.

Soak the gelatin in the lemon juice. Put the curd cheese into a bowl and beat in the egg yolks and honey. Gradually beat in the yoghurt and then 4 tbsp cherry juice. Stiffly whip the egg whites and fold them into the cheese mixture. Melt the gelatin over a low heat and mix it in quickly.

Line the sides of the cooled cake tin with greaseproof paper that you have oiled on both sides. Pour the cheese mixture into the tin and put it into the refrigerator to set.

Mix the arrowroot with 2 tbsp cherry syrup. Put the rest of the syrup into a saucepan and bring it to the boil. Stir in the arrowroot and cook, stirring, until the syrup becomes thick and transparent. Take it from the heat, add the cherries and allow to cool.

Just before serving, stand the tin on a jar and slide away the sides. Transfer the cheesecake to a serving plate, removing the tin base. Decorate the top with the cherries and thickened syrup.

Strawberry Shortcake Cheesecake

12 oz (350 g) strawberries
2 oz (50 g) shelled walnuts
6 oz (175 g) wholewheat flour
4 oz (125 g) butter or vegetable margarine
2 oz (50 g) Barbados sugar
½ oz (15 g) gelatin
1 tbsp honey
4 oz (125 g) low fat soft cheese
6 tbsp natural yoghurt
2 egg whites

Preheat the oven to 400°F (200°C/gas 6). Rub half the strawberries through a sieve.

Finely grind the walnuts and mix them with the flour. Cream the butter and beat in the sugar. Mix in the flour and walnuts and form the mixture into a dough. Press the dough into the base and sides of an 8 inch (20 cm) diameter tart tin. Bake for 15 minutes or until firm and biscuity. Cool the base completely and lift it out of the tin on to a flat plate.

Soak the gelatin in 4 tbsp warm water. Put the sieved strawberries into a saucepan and stir in the honey. Stir over a low heat until the honey dissolves. Melt the gelatin over a low heat and stir it into the strawberry purée. Cool the purée completely until it is on the point of setting.

Put the cheese into a bowl and gradually beat in the yoghurt. Beat in the cooled purée. Stiffly whip the egg whites and fold them into the strawberry mixture.

Spoon the mixture on top of the shortcake base. It should fill it completely and remain slightly piled up. Leave the shortcake in a cool place for the filling to set. Decorate the top with the remaining strawberries.

Pumpkin Curd Tart

This is a variation of American pumpkin pie. The yellow-gold filling tastes like a rich cheesecake.

> shortcrust pastry made with 8 oz (225 g)
>   wholewheat flour
> 1½ lb (675 g) slice pumpkin
> 4 oz (125 g) sugar-free apricot jam or
>   marmalade
> 4 oz (125 g) raisins
> 6 oz (175 g) curd cheese
> 3 oz (75 g) honey
> 3 eggs, beaten
> ¼ tsp ground mixed spice
> pinch ground mace

Preheat the oven to 400°F (200°C/gas 6). Cut the rind and pith from the pumpkin. Chop the flesh into ¾ inch (2 cm) dice and wrap it in lightly oiled foil. Bake for 40 minutes. Sieve it or mash it to a purée and leave to cool.

Turn the oven down to 350°F (180°C/gas 4). Line a 9 inch (23 cm) tart tin with the pastry. Spread the jam or marmalade over the base and sprinkle in the raisins in an even layer.

Beat the curd cheese with the honey and gradually beat in the eggs. Beat in the spices and stir in the pumpkin. Pour the mixture over the raisins and bake the tart for 45 minutes or until the filling is set and golden brown.

Healthy Mincemeat

Not only healthy, but the most delicious!

> 12 oz (350 g) Bramley apples
> 8 oz (225 g) figs
> 2 oz (50 g) almonds, blanched
> 4 fl oz (125 ml) brandy
> 8 oz (225 g) raisins
> 8 oz (225 g) sultanas
> 6 oz (175 g) currants
> 2 oz (50 g) candied peel (preferably bought in
>   one piece)
> 2 tsp ground mixed spice
> 1 oz (25 g) butter, melted

Peel, core and chop the apples. Chop the figs. Either put the apples, figs and almonds into a food processor with the brandy and work them to a rough minced mixture before turning them out into a bowl; or, mince together the apples, figs and almonds, put them into a bowl and mix in the brandy.

Add the raisins, sultanas and currants. Finely chop the peel and add it to the mixture together with the spice and butter. Mix well. Put into jars and seal.

Christmas Jelly Pudding

When is a pudding not a pudding? When it's a fruit jelly that looks like a pudding. This is pudding shaped, dark coloured and full of rich fruits. It makes a delicious light contrast after a rich Christmas dinner.

> 8 oz (225 g) muscatel raisins
> 8 oz (225 g) sultanas
> 4 oz (125 g) currants
> ¾ pint (425 ml) dry red wine
> 1 oz (25 g) gelatin
> oil for greasing

Put the raisins, sultanas, currants and wine into a saucepan. Bring them to simmering point and keep them at that temperature for 10 minutes. Take the pan from the heat.

In a small pan, soak the gelatin for 5 minutes in 4 tbsp of the hot wine. Melt it gently and pour it into the rest of the fruit and wine.

Oil a 1½ pint (850 ml) pudding basin and pour in the fruit and wine. Allow to cool and then put into the refrigerator to set.

To serve, dip the bowl into hot water and leave it for a few seconds. Cover it with a plate, invert it and lift the bowl away.

The Duffs' Favourite Christmas Pudding

> 2 oz (50 g) dried whole apricots
> 2½ oz (65 g) large seedless raisins
> 2½ oz (65 g) sultanas
> 2 oz (50 g) candied peel, finely chopped
> ¼ pint (150 ml) brandy
> 1 oz (25 g) almonds
> 1 small Bramley apple
> 1 medium carrot
> 1½ oz (40 g) wholewheat bread crumbs
> 1½ oz (40 g) wholewheat flour
> 2 oz (50 g) fresh beef suet

½ tsp baking powder
¼ tsp ground allspice
¼ tsp ground ginger
¼ nutmeg grated
pinch salt
1 egg, beaten
butter for greasing

Finely chop the apricots and put them into a bowl with the raisins, sultanas and peel. Fold in 8 tbsp brandy and leave them for 24 hours.

Blanch and shred the almonds, peel and grate the apple and grate the carrot. Mix these with the soaked fruit. Finely grate the suet.

Put the breadcrumbs and flour into a mixing bowl with the suet, baking powder, spices and salt. Mix in the fruit, beaten egg and remaining 2 tbsp brandy.

Butter a 1½ pint (850 ml) pudding basin. Put in the mixture, press it down and smooth the top. Cover the pudding with a layer of buttered greaseproof and foil (both with a pleat in the centre) and tie them down with string, making a handle for easy lifting. Bring a large saucepan of water to the boil, lower in the pudding and steam it for 4 hours, never letting it come off the boil. Lift out the pudding, let it cool completely, and replace the foil and greaseproof.

Before serving, boil it for a further 2 hours and serve it with brandy butter made with 8 oz (225 g) saltless butter, 4 oz (100 g) Barbados sugar and 4 tbsp brandy.

Alternative to brandy butter
8 oz (225 g) curd cheese
2 tbsp honey
4 tbsp brandy

Cream the cheese in a bowl. Beat in the honey and brandy. Chill for 1½ hours before serving.

Cold and fresh tasting, this makes a delicious contrast to the rich, hot pudding.

Wholewheat Baking

Baking is one of the most satisfying occupations I know. Of course, you can buy wholewheat bread, pastries, cakes and biscuits from many wholefood shops, supermarkets and small shops, but none ever seems to be as good as those that you make yourself. Also, when making baked goods at home you know that there are no preservatives added, you can use the fats and oils of your choice and not use too much sugar. Nothing is more pleasing than a homely pie, a tray of freshly baked cakes or a crusty brown loaf warm from the oven.

People are often doubtful about changing to wholewheat baking from baking with white flour. Will my bread be soggy and heavy? Will my pastry be like hard tack? Will my cakes be dull and flat? These are just a few of the many questions that I get asked. Well, if you are a competent cook and have always baked successfully with white flour there is no reason at all why you should have any trouble with wholewheat. If you are just beginning to bake and have no previous experience (or pre-judices), then start with the basics and work from there.

If you make pastry with the conventional recipe – half fat to flour and rubbed in with the fingers – you may well find that you will need more water than with white flour. Flours vary, some are drier than others, but you will need 4 to 6 tbsp to every 8 oz (225 g) wholewheat flour. However, I put this method aside long ago. All the time-consuming rubbing in is just not necessary. Use the all-in-one or what I call the fail-safe method (see page 169) and you will have perfect pastry in less than half the time. There really is no difference in flavour or texture. Another advantage is that this type of pastry is incredibly good tempered. You can roll it out, gather it all up together again and nobody will ever know. It will still be light and crisp. Use wholewheat pastry to make closed pies and quiches, sweet pies and sweet and savoury tarts.

Cakes made with wholewheat flour will obviously not be

light and airy, but they will rise and they have a definite flavour, not just one of air and sugar. If you have never made a whole-wheat cake before start with the basic Victoria sponge using 6 oz (175 g) each vegetable margarine or softened butter, whole-wheat flour and Barbados sugar plus 3 beaten eggs. This will help you to get the feel of your ingredients. Later you can experiment. Add honey instead of sugar and perhaps less of it. Use corn oil and a little water instead of the fat.

My recent experiments have been to replace all the sugar with cooked and puréed dried fruits. They have been extremely successful and the cakes are pleasantly sweet and light textured.

I always like to have a tea bread in the house. This is a cross between a sweet bread and a cake, made with only a small amount of fat and sweetener. Being semi-sweet they can be served plain or buttered, with cheese or spread with a sugar-free jam.

Scones are probably the easiest of all baked goods to make. Mixing and cooking can take less than 45 minutes. Make them plain or add sweet or savoury flavourings. Once you have made them with wholewheat flour you can try replacing a quarter of it with fine oatmeal or rye flour. For a crisp, nutty texture, you can add extra bran.

Once your scones are successful, then why not try bread? It is not as difficult or as time consuming as you might believe. For long periods of time it is in fact working away by itself, leaving you free to do other things. You have to mix it once, knead it twice and put it into the tins. Put like that, it sounds easy, and in actual fact it is. The main rules are: leave the yeast for long enough; let the bread rise for long enough; don't let it prove for too long; make sure the oven is up to temperature before you put in the bread.

Follow the basic recipe and, when you feel it is right, go on to more complicated things such as sweetened breads, savoury breads and rolls. I have included my recipe for muffins as they are fun to toast by the fire in the winter.

Most of the biscuits that I make are semi-sweet so that they are pleasant to munch over a cup of herb tea mid-morning without filling you up. I sometimes use concentrated apple juice as a sweetener. It is not too rich and has a light effect.

Failsafe Wholewheat Pastry

> 8 oz (225 g) wholewheat flour
> pinch fine sea salt
> 5 oz (150 g) vegetable margarine or butter, softened

Put the flour and salt into a mixing bowl and make a well in the centre. Put the margarine or butter into the well. Use a soft vegetable margarine straight from the packet. Butter must be very soft, almost melting is best.

Add 4 tbsp cold water. Stir with a fork or round bladed knife until everything comes together in a dough. It is best to use your fingers for the final pressing together.

Coat the dough in a light dusting of flour and leave it in a cool place for 30 minutes before using.

Onion, Cheese and Bacon Quiche

This makes a substantial main meal when served hot. Cold, it is good for lunches and picnics.

> Shortcrust pastry made with 8 oz (225 g)
>   wholewheat flour, plus 2 tsp dried mixed herbs
> 4 large onions, thinly sliced
> 4 oz (125 g) lean bacon
> 3 eggs
> ¼ pint (150 ml) milk
> 4 tbsp chopped parsley
> 1 tbsp chopped thyme
> 1 tbsp chopped marjoram
> 5 oz (150 g) Cheddar cheese, grated

Preheat the oven to 400°F (200°C/gas 6). Bring a saucepan of water to the boil. Add the onions and cook them for 5 minutes. Drain. Grill and chop the bacon.

Roll out the pastry and line a 10 inch (25 cm) tart tin. Put the bacon in the bottom and then the onions.

Beat the eggs. Beat in the milk, herbs and 4 oz (125 g) of the cheese. Pour the mixture over the onions, making sure that the cheese is evenly distributed. Scatter the remaining cheese over the top.

Bake the quiche for 30 minutes or until the filling has browned and set.

Honeyed Apple Chimneys

These spiced apple tarts can be served hot or cold.

> *Pastry*
> 7 oz (200 g) wholewheat flour
> pinch salt
> 1 egg, separated
> 4 oz (125 g) butter, softened, or vegetable margarine
> 2 tbsp honey
>
> *Filling*
> 1 medium Bramley apple
> 3 oz (75 g) sultanas
> 1 tsp ground cinnamon
> 2 tbsp honey

Preheat the oven to 400°F (200°C/gas 6). Put the flour on a worktop. Scatter on the salt and make a well in the centre. Put in the egg yolk, butter and honey. Pound in the flour from the edges with your fingertips so you eventually have a ball of smooth dough. Let it rest, covered with a cloth, while you prepare the filling.

Peel, core and very finely chop the apple. Mix it in a bowl with the sultanas, cinnamon and honey. Roll out the pastry and stamp out an equal number of 2½ inch (6 cm) and 2 inch (5 cm) rounds. With an apple corer or very small pastry cutter stamp out circles in the centre of the smaller rounds. Use the trimmings to make more rounds. Line floured tartlet tins with the large rounds. Put in a portion of the apple mixture and cover it with a small round. Press the sides down, carefully, so you have small chimney or volcano shapes.

Brush the tartlets with the egg white and bake them for 15 minutes so they are golden brown.

Either eat them hot or cool them on a wire rack.

Honey and Molasses Parkin

This is based on a recipe from my grandmother's cookery book.

> 10 oz (300 g) wholewheat flour
> 6 oz (175 g) medium oatmeal
> 1 tsp bicarbonate of soda
> 1 tsp ground ginger
> 1 tsp ground mace
> little freshly grated nutmeg
> 2 oz (50 g) candied peel, finely chopped
> 6 oz (175 g) butter or vegetable margarine plus
>   extra for greasing
> 8 oz (225 g) honey
> 8 oz (225 g) molasses

Preheat the oven to 350°F (180°C/gas 4). Put the flour and oatmeal into a bowl. Add the bicarbonate of soda, ginger, mace, nutmeg and candied peel and mix well. Make a well in the centre. Put the butter, honey and molasses into a saucepan and gently melt them together over a low heat. Pour them into the flour and oatmeal and mix everything together well.

Put the mixture into a well greased 8 × 11 inch (20 × 28 cm) baking tin and bake it for 40 minutes or until firm. Cool it in the tin until lukewarm. Turn it out and cut it into small squares.

Don't expect parkin to be light and risen like an ordinary cake, in fact it may even sink a little in the middle. It should be chewy, tasty and full of goodness. Never eat parkin straight away. Keep it for at least two days in an airtight container. My grandmother's old recipe book recommends that it be kept for two weeks. It is therefore an excellent make-in-advance recipe.

Carob Cup Cakes

Children love these cup cakes. They have almost a caramel flavour and a gooey texture.

> 6 oz (175 g) wholewheat flour
> 1 oz (25 g) carob powder, sieved

2 tsp baking powder
6 oz (175 g) vegetable margarine
6 oz (175 g) dark Barbados sugar
3 eggs, beaten
margarine for greasing

Icing
4 oz (125 g) curd cheese
2 tbsp honey
2 tbsp carob powder

Preheat the oven to 350°F (180°C/gas 4). Toss the flour with the carob powder and baking powder. Cream the margarine with the sugar. Beat in about 2 tbsp of the flour mixture and then a little of the beaten eggs. Continue adding flour and eggs alternately until all are used up and the mixture is smooth.

Grease two trays of 12 bun tins and half fill the moulds with the mixture. Bake for 15 minutes, or until firm. Allow to cool completely on wire racks.

To make the icing, cream the curd cheese in a bowl. Beat in the honey. Put the carob powder into a small bowl and stir in 3 tbsp hot water so you have a smooth, stiff paste. Spoon over the cakes.

Corn Oil Orange Cake

Beaten egg whites give this cake a light, spongy texture.

6 oz (175 g) wholewheat flour
pinch salt
1 tsp baking powder
grated rind and juice 1 large orange
5 oz (150 g) light Barbados sugar
4 fl oz (125 g) corn oil
2 eggs, separated

Filling
4 oz (125 g) curd cheese
3 tbsp sugar-free marmalade

Preheat the oven to 350°F (180°C/gas 4). Put the flour into a bowl with the salt, baking powder, orange rind and sugar. Mix them together. Make a well in the centre and pour in the oil. Make the juice of the orange up to 6 tbsp with water. Add it to the well and put in the egg yolks. Beat with a wooden spoon to a fairly stiff mixture. Stiffly whip the egg whites and fold them in.

Divide the mixture between two oiled 7 inch (18 cm) diameter sponge tins. Bake the cakes for 20 minutes until they are firm and have shrunk slightly from the sides of the tin. Turn them on to wire racks to cool.

To make the filling, beat the cheese to a cream and beat in the marmalade 1 tbsp at a time. Sandwich the cakes together with the filling.

Date Muffins

> 8 oz (225 g) fresh dates, or semi-dried if unavailable
> 8 oz (225 g) wholewheat flour
> 2 tbsp bran
> 2 tbsp wheatgerm
> 1 tsp bicarbonate of soda
> 3 tbsp oil plus extra for greasing
> 2 tbsp honey
> 2 tbsp molasses
> 1 egg, beaten
> 8 fl oz (225 ml) milk

Preheat the oven to 375°F (190°C/gas 5). Grease about 18 individual bun tins.

Stone, skin and chop the dates. In a mixing bowl, combine the flour, bran, wheatgerm and bicarbonate of soda. Make a well in the centre. Put the oil, honey and molasses into a saucepan and melt them over a low heat. Pour them into the flour. Add the egg and milk and beat to make a thick batter. Mix in the dates.

Spoon the mixture into the prepared tins. Bake the muffins for 15 minutes or until they are firm and risen.

Apple and Date Cake

Even the person with the sweetest tooth won't be able to tell that this cake doesn't have sugar in it. It is deliciously sweet and surprisingly light.

2 oz (50 g) dried apple rings
4 oz (125 g) stoned dates
½ pint (275 ml) natural apple juice
6 oz (175 g) flour
1 tsp bicarbonate of soda
6 tbsp corn oil plus extra for greasing
2 eggs, beaten

Preheat the oven to 350°F (180°C/gas 4). Put the apple rings, dates and apple juice into a saucepan. Bring to the boil. Take the pan from the heat and soak the fruit for 4 hours. Drain, reserving the juice. Liquidize the fruits with 6 tbsp of the juice.

Put the flour and bicarbonate of soda into a bowl and make a well in the centre. Add the liquidized fruits and the corn oil and gradually beat in the flour from the sides of the well. Add the eggs and beat until the mixture is smooth.

Put the mixture into an oiled 8 inch (20 cm) diameter cake tin and bake the cake for 20 minutes or until it is golden and firm to the touch.

Rich Fruit Cake

Serve this plainly or decorate it for birthdays or Christmas.

4 oz (125 g) prunes
¼ pint (150 ml) prune juice
¼ pint (150 ml) apple juice
4 oz (125 g) stoned dates
8 oz (225 g) wholewheat flour
1 tsp ground mixed spice
6 oz (125 g) vegetable margarine or butter, softened
1 medium carrot, finely grated

4 eggs, beaten
6 oz (175 g) sultanas
6 oz (175 g) raisins

Soak the prunes in the prune and apple juices for 4 hours. Drain, reserving the juice. Stone and finely chop the prunes. Finely chop the dates. Put them into a saucepan with ¼ pint (150 ml) of the reserved juice. Bring to the boil and simmer for 5 minutes. Cool and liquidize them.

Heat the oven to 300°F (160°C/gas 2). Mix the flour with the spice. In a large mixing bowl, cream the margarine and beat in the carrot. Beat the eggs, alternately with the flour. Beat in the liquidized dried fruits and then the sultanas and raisins. Put the mixture into a greased 8 inch (20 cm) diameter cake tin.

Bake the cake for 1 hour or until a skewer inserted in the centre comes out clean. Cool it in the tin for 5 minutes and turn it on to a wire rack to cool completely.

DECORATIONS

Spread the top lightly with honey or with sugar-free apricot jam. Stick on blanched almonds, walnut halves or halved glacé cherries.

Cut out a decoration, such as a flower or a number for the age of a child, from a circular template. Lay the template in the centre of the cake. Spread honey or sugar-free apricot jam over the hole and press ground almonds thickly over the top.

Make an almond paste by mixing 4 oz (125 g) ground almonds with 2 tbsp honey and 2 tbsp concentrated apple juice. Divide it into several portions and colour each one with a different food colouring. This can be made into stand-up shapes, or rolled out to cover the cake completely, or rolled out and stamped into shapes such as Christmas trees and stars. When working with it, damp your hands, work surface and rolling pin with cold water.

Mixed Fruit Tea Bread

This is a moist, spicy tea bread, relying solely on the dried fruits for sweetness. Eat it plain or buttered.

> 1 lb (450 g) wholewheat flour
> 2 tsp bicarbonate of soda
> 1 tsp salt
> 1 tsp ground mixed spice
> 4 oz (125 g) butter
> 4 oz (125 g) stoned dates, finely chopped
> 4 oz (125 g) sultanas
> 4 oz (125 g) raisins
> 3 eggs, beaten
> ½ pint (275 ml) natural yoghurt

Preheat the oven to 350°F (180°C/gas 4). Put the flour into a mixing bowl with the bicarbonate of soda, salt and spices. Rub in the butter and then mix in the dried fruits. Make a well in the centre and pour in the eggs and yoghurt. Mix well to make a moist dough.

Put the mixture into a buttered, 2 lb (900 g) loaf tin and bake it for 1 hour, or until a skewer inserted in the centre comes out clean. If, after the first 30 minutes the bread looks as though it will brown too quickly, cover the top with a double layer of damp greaseproof paper. Turn the bread on to a wire rack to cool completely.

Basic Scone Mixture

Scones and soda bread are always best eaten on the day that you make them.

> 8 oz (225 g) wholewheat flour
> ½ tsp fine sea salt
> ½ tsp bicarbonate of soda
> 1 oz (25 g) butter, vegetable margarine or soft lard

¼ pint (150 ml) sour milk, natural yoghurt or
buttermilk, or fresh milk with ½ tsp cream of
tartar added

Preheat the oven to 400°F (200°C/gas 6). Put the flour into a
bowl with the salt and bicarbonate of soda. Rub in the fat. Make
a well in the centre and pour in the liquid. Mix everything to a
dough and knead it lightly until smooth.

The dough can be made into a thick round and a cross-cut
made in the centre. Bake it on a floured baking sheet for 30
minutes. This is soda bread.

Or roll it into a 1 inch (2.5 cm) thick round. Lay it on a baking
sheet and score the top into 12 wedges. Bake it for 25 minutes.

Or stamp out round scones or cut square or triangular shaped
scones. Lay them on a baking sheet and bake them for 20
minutes or until just beginning to colour.

Savoury Cheese Scones

These savoury scones can be eaten plain, spread with butter or
butter and Marmite, or topped with cheese. They are best eaten
on the day that they are made.

1 lb (450 g) wholewheat flour
1 tsp bicarbonate of soda
1 tsp cream of tartar
1 tsp sea salt
1½ oz (40 g) butter or vegetable margarine
2 oz (50 g) farmhouse Cheddar cheese, grated
2 tbsp chopped parsley
1 tbsp chopped thyme
2 tbsp chopped chives
½ pint (275 ml) buttermilk or natural yoghurt
2 tbsp Worcestershire sauce

Preheat the oven to 400°F (200°C/gas 6). Put the flour into a
bowl with the soda, cream of tartar and salt and rub in the butter
or margarine. Lightly toss in the cheese and herbs with your
fingers. Make a well in the centre of the mixture and pour in the

buttermilk or yoghurt and the Worcestershire sauce. Mix everything to a dough and roll it out to a thickness of ¾ inch (2 cm). Stamp it into rounds with a 2 inch (5 cm) biscuit cutter.

Put the scones on to a floured baking sheet and bake them for 20 minutes. Lift them on to a wire rack to cool.

Apple Scones

These spicy scones are semi-sweet and apple flavoured.

> 2 oz (50 g) dried apple rings
> ¼ pint (150 ml) prune juice or apple juice
> 8 oz (225 g) wholewheat flour
> ½ tsp bicarbonate of soda
> ½ tsp fine sea salt
> ½ tsp ground cloves
> 1½ oz (40 g) butter or vegetable margarine
> ¼ pint (150 ml) sour milk, natural yoghurt or
> buttermilk

Preheat the oven to 400°F (200°C/gas 6). Soak the apple rings in the prune juice and ¼ pint (150 ml) water for 4 hours. Drain and liquidize them. Put the flour into a mixing bowl with the bicarbonate of soda, salt and ground cloves. Rub in the butter or margarine. Make a well in the centre and add the yoghurt and apples. Mix everything to a dough.

Roll out the dough to a thickness of ¾ inch (2 cm) and stamp it into 2 inch (5 cm) rounds with a biscuit cutter. Lay them on a floured baking sheet and bake for 20 minutes. Lift them on to a wire rack to cool.

Wholewheat Bread

> 1 oz (25 g) fresh yeast or ½ oz (15 g) dried yeast plus
>   1 tsp honey
> 2 tsp sea salt
> 1 lb (450 g) wholewheat flour plus extra for kneading
> oil for greasing
> 1 egg, beaten, for glaze (optional)

Put ¼ pt (150 ml) warm water into a bowl. Crumble in the fresh yeast; or sprinkle in the dried yeast and stir in the honey. Leave the yeast in a warm place to froth. The fresh yeast need only just begin to bubble (about 10 minutes); the dried needs to be very frothy (about 20 minutes).

In a jug, dissolve the salt in ¼ pt (150 ml) warm water. Put the flour into a mixing bowl and make a well in the centre. Pour in the yeast mixture and mix in a little of the flour from the edges of the well. Pour in the salt mixture and mix everything to a rough, lumpy dough.

Turn the dough on to a floured work surface. With floured hands, knead it until it is smooth.

Return the dough to the bowl. Make a cross-cut in the top. Cover the bowl with a clean, dry tea towel and leave it in a warm place for about 1 hour or until the dough has doubled in size.

In some books you may find instructions to put the bowl inside a greased polythene bag. I personally find this too messy and tiresome and besides I can never find a bag big enough. However, it does provide a nice warm container in which the yeast can get to work.

Preheat the oven to 400°F (200°C/gas 6). Oil a 2 lb (900 g) loaf tin. Turn the dough on to the floured work surface again and knead it lightly. Put it into the prepared tin and press it down very lightly. Brush the top with beaten egg. Put the loaf in a warm place and cover it with the tea towel again. Leave it until it has risen about ½ inch (1.5 cm) above the sides of the tin.

Bake the loaf for 50 minutes, or until it is golden brown and sounds hollow when tapped. Turn it on to a wire rack to cool.

Ideally, the loaf should be left for 12 hours before being eaten. At least wait (if you can!) until it is completely cold.

ALTERNATIVES

Scatter cracked wheat, poppy seeds or sesame seeds over the beaten egg glaze.

Slash the top after glazing, either with one long cut down the centre or with three diagonal cuts.

Make the loaf into a round or bloomer shape and bake it on a baking tray.

Divide the dough into two, use two 1 lb (450 g) bread tins and bake for 40 minutes.

Bake in one large or two small earthenware bread pots.

Divide the dough into 12 pieces, make them into round rolls and bake them for 20 minutes.

Use 8 oz (225 g) rye or barley flour with 8 oz (225 g) wholewheat flour.

Use 4 oz (125 g) fine oatmeal with 12 oz (350 g) wholewheat flour.

Index

MORE ABOUT PENGUINS, PELICANS
AND PUFFINS

COOKERY AND GARDENING
IN PENGUINS

☐ *Italian Food* **Elizabeth David** £3.50

'The great book on Italian cooking in English' – Hugh Johnson. 'Certainly the best book we know dealing not only with the food but with the wines of Italy' – *Wine and Food*

☐ *An Invitation to Indian Cooking* **Madhur Jaffrey** £2.95

A witty, practical and irresistible handbook on Indian cooking by the presenter of the highly successful BBC television series.

☐ *The Pastry Book* **Rosemary Wadey** £2.95

From Beef Wellington to Treacle Tart and Cream-filled Eclairs – here are sweet and savoury recipes for all occasions, plus expert advice that should give you winning results every time.

☐ *The Cottage Garden* **Anne Scott-James** £4.95

'Her history is neatly and simply laid out; well-stocked with attractive illustrations' – *The Times*. 'The garden book I have most enjoyed reading in the last few years' – *Observer*

☐ *Chinese Food* **Kenneth Lo** £1.75

The popular, step-by-step introduction to the philosophy, practice, menus and delicious recipes of Chinese cooking.

☐ *The Cuisine of the Rose* **Mireille Johnston** £5.95

Classic French cooking from Burgundy and Lyonnais, explained with the kind of flair, atmosphere and enthusiasm that only the most exciting cookbooks possess.

PENGUINS ON HEALTH, SPORT AND KEEPING FIT

☐ **Audrey Eyton's F-Plus** £1.95

F-Plan menus for women who lunch at work * snack eaters * keen cooks * freezer-owners * busy dieters using convenience foods * overweight children * drinkers and non-drinkers. 'Your short-cut to the most sensational diet of the century' – *Daily Express*

☐ **The F-Plan Calorie Counter and Fibre Chart Audrey Eyton** £1.95

An indispensable companion to the F-Plan diet. High-fibre fresh, canned and packaged foods are listed, there's a separate chart for drinks, *plus* a wonderful selection of effortless F-Plan meals.

☐ **The Parents A–Z Penelope Leach** £6.95

From the expert author of *Baby & Child*, this skilled, intelligent and comprehensive guide is by far the best reference book currently available for parents, whether your children are six months, six or sixteen years.

☐ **Woman's Experience of Sex Sheila Kitzinger** £5.95

Fully illustrated with photographs and line drawings, this book explores the riches of women's sexuality at every stage of life. 'A book which any mother could confidently pass on to her daughter and her partner too' – *Sunday Times*

☐ **Alternative Medicine Andrew Stanway** £3.25

From Acupuncture and Alexander Technique to Macrobiotics and Yoga, Dr Stanway provides an informed and objective guide to thirty-two therapies in alternative medicine.

☐ **Pregnancy Dr Jonathan Scher and Carol Dix** £2.95

Containing the most up-to-date information on pregnancy – the effects of stress, sexual intercourse, drugs, diet, late maternity and genetic disorders – this book is an invaluable and reassuring guide for prospective parents.

PENGUIN CROSSWORD BOOKS

☐ *The Penguin Jumbo Book of the Sun Crosswords*	£2.50
☐ *The Second Penguin Jumbo Book of the Sun Crosswords*	£2.50
☐ *The Ninth Penguin Book of the Sun Crosswords*	£1.95
☐ *The Eighth Penguin Book of the Sun Crosswords*	£1.95
☐ *The Seventh Penguin Book of the Sun Crosswords*	£1.50
☐ *The Sixth Penguin Book of the Sun Crosswords*	£1.25
☐ *The Daily Telegraph Sixteenth Crossword Puzzle Book*	£1.50
☐ *The Daily Telegraph Fiftieth Anniversary Crossword Puzzle Book*	£1.50
☐ *The Daily Telegraph Eighth Crossword Puzzle Book*	£1.50
☐ *The Seventh Penguin Book of The Sunday Times Crosswords*	£1.75
☐ *The Fifth Penguin Book of The Times Crosswords*	£1.75
☐ *The Penguin Bumper Book of Standard Two-in-One Crossword Puzzles*	£2.50

These books should be available at all good bookshops or news-agents, but if you live in the UK or the Republic of Ireland and have difficulty in getting to a bookshop, they can be ordered by post. Please indicate the titles required and fill in the form below.

NAME _____ BLOCK CAPITALS

ADDRESS _____

_____

_____

Enclose a cheque or postal order payable to The Penguin Bookshop to cover the total price of books ordered, plus 50p for postage. Readers in the Republic of Ireland should send £IR equivalent to the sterling prices, plus 67p for postage. Send to: The Penguin Bookshop, 54/56 Bridlesmith Gate, Nottingham, NG1 2GP.

You can also order by phoning (0602) 599295, and quoting your Barclaycard or Access number.

Every effort is made to ensure the accuracy of the price and availability of books at the time of going to press, but it is sometimes necessary to increase prices and in these circumstances retail prices may be shown on the covers of books which may differ from the prices shown in this list or elsewhere. This list is not an offer to supply any book.

This order service is only available to residents in the UK and the Republic of Ireland.

● ● ●